Table of Contents

About the Author

Sue Dawson knows food! For twenty-two years she was the food editor for *The Columbus Dispatch* in Columbus, Ohio, and prior to that she was the Home Editor for the *Ohio Farmer* magazine and an assistant publications editor at Ohio State University. Sue is a graduate of Kansas State University. Now retired, Sue resides in Columbus, Ohio and Phoenix, Arizona.

The author would like to acknowledge the following sources which provided invaluable information on the culinary history of the twentieth century:

The Food Chronology: A Food Lover's Compendium of Events and Anecdotes, From Prehistory to the Present, by James Trager, Henry Holt Reference Book, Henry Holt and Company, New York, 1995.

The American Century Cookbook: The Most Popular Recipes of the 20th Century, by Jean Anderson, Clarkson Potter/Publishers, New York, 1997.

Fashionable Food: Seven Decades of Food Fads, by Sylvia Lovegren, Macmillan, New York 1995.

Culinary History Timeline and The Food Timeline, sponsored by the Morris County Library, NJ

Dining Through the Decades, sponsored by Leite's Culinaria.

Twentieth Century Timeline Edibles & Quaffables.

Unless otherwise indicated in the text, the recipes are the author's creations or from her files. Information and inspiration, however, came from cookbooks, websites, magazines and newspapers too numerous to list.

Portions of this book originally appeared in *The Columbus Dispatch,* Columbus, Ohio and are used here with permission of *The Columbus Dispatch.*

Printed in USA, by G&R Publishing Co. Waverly, IA 50677

Published By:

Products

507 Industrial Street
Waverly, IA 50677

ISBN-13: 978-1-56383-331-1
ISBN-10: 1-56383-331-X
Item #7032

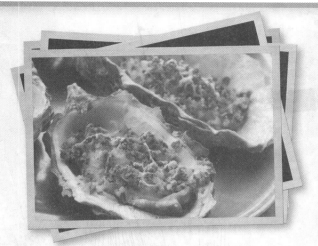

1900 to 1909

Life was good at the turn of the century. Dinner parties among the well-to-do were opulent, featuring 12 to 18 courses, made possible by full-time cooks and hired waiters.

Cocktails, served in thimble-sized glasses, began to be offered early in the 1900s, but wine – one for each course – was de rigueur.

Dinners often began with oysters, then a clear soup. They might be followed with dishes such as poached salmon, sweetbreads, fillet of beef, lamb chops, creamed chicken, roasted fowl, boiled potatoes and asparagus. Dessert might feature molded ice cream, cakes and fruit, followed by coffee and tea.

Illustrious restaurants, including Delmonico's in New York City and Antoine's in New Orleans, already were in high gear. Among dishes they introduced were Delmonico potatoes, oysters Rockefeller and soufflé potatoes, which remained popular throughout the 20th century.

Although city dwellers could sample pompano en papillote and crêpes Suzette in high-class restaurants, most Americans lived on farms or in small communities.

Housewives (as homemakers were called then) cooked on coal or wood stoves in kitchens equipped with an icebox, worktable and freestanding cupboard. Produce came from the root cellar or the garden, butter from a churn, eggs from hens penned in the back yard. Farm families butchered their own cattle and hogs, smoked their own bacon and made their own lard.

One thing the rich and common man shared was a sweet tooth. Sugar consumption was around 65 pounds per capita, used in everything from the simple Blanc Mange to the elegant Baked Alaska. Chocolate lovers had a heyday, too. Recipes for devil's food cake, brownies and fudge began appearing around this time.

Meanwhile, a countermovement to the era's culinary indulgence was flourishing. Promoting food for health's sake, the movement began in the late 1800s by health gurus such as John Harvey Kellogg, C.W. Post and Wilbur Olin Atwater.

Kellogg, a doctor and vegetarian who opened the Battle Creek Sanitarium in Michigan, created a cold breakfast cereal called Corn Flakes. It was intended to replace meat on the breakfast table.

Post, a former patient at the sanitarium, followed soon after with his own health food, called Grape-Nuts.

Atwater, a chemist, was one of this country's first nutrition scientists. He taught the public the concept of the calorie and about the nutritive values of foods. He also sought to educate consumers about eating correctly. Food should be considered a fuel and a symbol of morality, he preached, not something to be enjoyed.

About the same time, a new method of "scientific cooking" was developed, mostly by women reformers who worked to standardize measurements and develop diets and menus based on nutrients and calories. Called domestic science (later home economics), this movement also investigated food adulteration and spoilage.

Cooking by numbers also had a proponent in Fanny Merritt Farmer, the principal of the Boston Cooking School at the turn of the century.

Farmer, who emphasized simple food, used standardized cups and spoons for measuring ingredients instead of vague descriptions in older recipes, such as butter "the size of a hen's egg" or cookie dough formed into "walnut-sized balls."

Her uncomplicated recipes found a willing audience in housewives without domestic help who – sans electric mixers, refrigerators, Pyrex dishes or Crisco – spent most of their waking hours in the kitchen.

Oysters Rockefeller

¾ pound fresh spinach
1 bunch green onions, including tops
¼ cup chopped celery leaves
¼ cup chopped parsley
2 tablespoons chopped fresh herbs, such
  as chervil, tarragon or thyme, optional
1½ cups (3 sticks) butter
2 tablespoons Pernod
Salt, pepper and hot pepper sauce to taste
Rock salt
3 dozen oysters on the half shell

Created in 1899 by Jules Alciatore, the second-generation owner of Antoine's restaurant in New Orleans, the dish was named after the wealthy Rockefeller family because of its rich flavor. Although the original recipe never has been revealed, Alciatore's great-grandson Roy F. Guste Jr. has said the dish never contained spinach, which most modern recipes do.

By hand or in a food processor, finely mince the spinach, onions, celery leaves, parsley and, if desired, the fresh herbs. Melt the butter and stir in the minced greens, Pernod and seasonings.

Heat broiler. Fill shallow pans, such as pie pans, with rock salt. Place oysters on the salt. Top each oyster with some of the spinach mixture. Place under the broiler and broil until heated through, 5 to 6 minutes. Makes 6 servings.

1900-1909 · FACTS · 1900-1909

Tuna was first put into a can.

Sugar was selling for 4¢ a pound, eggs for 14¢ per dozen and butter for 25¢ a pound.

1900

Senate Bean Soup

1 pound dry navy beans
Water
1 meaty ham bone or 2 pork hocks
1 medium onion, chopped
1 cup mashed potatoes, optional,
  see note below
Salt and pepper

Although stories about this soup vary, many sources credit House Speaker Joe Cannon's angry outburst for the soup's long and continuing run in House dining rooms. A staple on the menu, it was omitted one summer day. The Speaker is said to have stormed, "Thunderation, I had my mouth set for bean soup. From now on, hot or cold, rain, snow or shine. I want it on the menu every day."

Senator Knute Nelson reportedly made a similar order that the soup be served in the Senate dining room every day. Later, a decree was made that the beans must be Michigan white beans.

Soak beans in water to cover overnight. Drain and place in a large soup pot with 3 quarts water, the ham bone and onion. Cover and simmer until beans are tender, 2½ to 3 hours. Remove ham bone. When cool enough to handle, remove meat from bone, chop meat and return to the beans. Stir in potatoes, if desired, and salt and pepper to taste. Heat through. Makes about 6 servings.

Note: Potatoes were added to thicken the soup. They can be omitted, and the soup thickened by mashing some of the cooked beans and stirring them back into the soup.

Minnesota Valley Canning Co. in Le Sueur began packing peas and corn in cans.

1900·1909 • FACTS • 1900·1909

Honeydew melons were introduced in the United States.

Waldorf Salad

1 cup diced unpeeled red apples
1 cup sliced celery
½ cup coarsely chopped walnuts
1 cup mayonnaise, or to taste

In a mixing bowl, combine apples, celery and walnuts. Lightly fold in mayonnaise, until ingredients are coated. Makes about 4 servings.

Created just before the turn of the century at the Waldorf-Astoria Hotel in New York, this salad maintains its popularity even today. Originally a simple combination of chopped apples, celery and mayonnaise, the recipe was later doctored with nuts and sometimes with marshmallows, pineapple and/or dates.

Auguste Escoffier published the classic Le Guide Culinaire *– a tome with 1,000 recipes. Escoffier, of London's Carlton Hotel, says a sauce should fit the meat or fish it's served with, coffee should only be served at the end of the meal and fruit is the only appropriate food to serve after pastries.*

Delmonico Potatoes

*Said to have been
created at Delmonico's
restaurant in New
York, the dish in
modern times is simply
called "Au Gratin
Potatoes."*

1 tablespoon butter or margarine
½ cup fine dry bread crumbs
2 tablespoons butter or margarine
2 tablespoons flour
2 cups milk
½ teaspoon salt
⅛ teaspoon white pepper
1 cup shredded Cheddar or American cheese
2 cups cold boiled potatoes, cubed

Melt 1 tablespoon butter. Stir in bread crumbs until coated. Set aside. In a medium saucepan, melt 2 tablespoons butter. Stir in flour, whisking until bubbly. Slowly add milk, stirring constantly, until thickened and bubbly. Add salt, pepper and cheese. Remove from heat and stir until cheese is melted. Fold in potatoes thoroughly

Transfer to a shallow baking dish. Sprinkle bread crumbs on top. Bake in 400° oven about 20 minutes or until mixture is bubbly and lightly browned. Makes about 4 servings.

*The country's first pizzeria opened
in New York City.*

∽∘∽

*James Beard, "The Father
of American Gastronomy"
and author of innumerable
cookbooks, was born in 1904.*

1900·1909 · 1900·1909
FACTS

Spanish Rice

1 cup long-grain rice
4 slices bacon
⅓ cup chopped onion
⅓ cup chopped green pepper
1 can (14.5 ounces) chopped tomatoes,
  undrained
1 teaspoon salt
¼ teaspoon pepper

Originally made with chicken or salt pork at the turn of the century, Spanish Rice as it is known today was most popular as a meatless dish during World War II.

Cook rice in water according to package directions until tender. In a frying pan, cook bacon until crisp. Remove bacon. Sauté onion and green pepper in bacon drippings until tender. Add rice, tomatoes and seasonings. Crumble bacon and stir into pan. Transfer to a 1½-quart baking dish and bake uncovered at 350° until bubbly, about 30 minutes. Makes 6 to 8 servings.

The Jungle, *by Upton Beall Sinclair, exposed unsanitary conditions in U.S. meatpacking plants. Many readers became vegetarians; Congress was led to pass the Meat Inspection Act the following year.*

Two timesavers for cooks — the electric toaster and drip coffeemakers — made their debut.

Chicken à la King

3 tablespoons butter or margarine
½ cup chopped green pepper
1 cup sliced mushrooms
4 tablespoons flour
1 cup chicken stock
1 cup light cream or half & half
1½ cups cooked cubed chicken
¼ cup slivered pimentos
Salt and pepper to taste

Another recipe created in the famed Delmonico's, this creamed chicken dish caught on with home cooks. Recipes for it were commonly found in cookbooks from early in the century through the '50s.

Melt butter in a medium frying pan. Add green pepper and mushrooms and cook until tender. Stir in flour until smooth. Slowly stir in stock and cream and cook, stirring constantly, until smooth and bubbly. Add cooked chicken and pimentos. Taste and add salt and pepper as needed. Serve over toast or biscuits or in pastry shells. Makes 4 to 6 servings.

1900-1909
FACTS
1900-1909

The Frugal Gourmet's Culinary Handbook *appeared in print with 4,000 recipes, 70 of them for consommé.*

⸎

The first recipe for devil's food cake appeared in print.

Lady Baltimore Cake

¼ cup (½ stick) butter, softened
¼ cup vegetable shortening
1½ cups sugar
2½ cups cake flour
2½ teaspoons baking powder
1 teaspoon salt
1 cup milk
1 teaspoon vanilla
4 egg whites

This cake gets its name from the novel Lady Baltimore, *written by Owen Wister in 1906. Wister, the story goes, was served the cake in the Women's Exchange tea room in Charleston, SC, and was so enthralled with it he decided to write about it. The novelist mentions only nuts in the filling, but figs and raisins are traditional. A white cake is the usual base.*

Grease and flour two 9-inch round cake pans. Heat oven to 350°.

Cake: Cream together the butter, shortening and sugar at low speed until light, smooth and fluffy. Sift together the flour, baking powder and salt. Mix milk and vanilla. Add flour mixture to creamed mixture alternately with liquid, beginning and ending with flour.

Beat egg whites at high speed until stiff peaks form; fold into batter. Divide batter equally between prepared pans. Bake 30 to 35 minutes or until no imprint is left when layers are lightly touched in the middle. Cool 10 minutes, then turn out and cool completely on cake rack.

Filling and Frosting

2½ cups sugar
1 tablespoon light corn syrup
1 cup water
3 egg whites
1 teaspoon vanilla
½ cup chopped walnuts
⅓ cup raisins
⅓ cup finely chopped figs

Combine sugar, corn syrup and water in a heavy saucepan and heat over medium heat to 242°. While syrup is cooking, beat egg whites at high speed until stiff enough to hold a peak. Pour syrup slowly over egg whites, beating constantly. Add vanilla. Continue beating until mixture will hold its shape.

Combine nuts and fruits in a small bowl. Add just enough frosting to bind; use between the layers. Cover top and sides of cake with the remaining frosting.

1900

Devil's Food Cake

½ cup vegetable shortening
1½ cups sugar
2 eggs
1¾ cups sifted cake flour
1¼ teaspoons baking soda
½ teaspoon salt
⅓ cup cocoa
1 cup milk
1 teaspoon vanilla

Heat oven to 350°. Grease and flour two 8- or 9-inch round cake pans. In mixer bowl, beat shortening and sugar until light and fluffy. Beat in eggs, one at a time.

Sift together the flour, soda, salt and cocoa. Add to the creamed mixture alternately with the milk, beginning and ending with the dry ingredients, beating after each addition only until combined. Stir in vanilla. Turn into prepared pans and bake 35 to 40 minutes for 8-inch pans, 30 to 35 minutes for 9-inch pans or until a pick inserted into the center comes out clean.

Cool in pans 10 minutes, then turn out onto wire racks to cool completely. Frost as desired.

Several theories surround this cake's name. One is that the chocolate cake is so rich, it's wicked or devilish. Another is that it was a word play on opposites: the light and airy angel food cake and the dark, rich devil's food. Still another relates to the red color of the cake, reminiscent of a devil's cape.

The red color originally was thought to be caused by a chemical reaction between early varieties of cocoa and baking soda. Later cooks added large amounts of red food coloring, a practice discouraged in the '70s when a link was made between certain food dyes and cancer.

The cake was first noted in cookbooks around the turn of the century. It's generally iced with Seven-Minute Icing (see page 36) or a chocolate buttercream.

Blanc Mange

⅔ cup sugar
3 tablespoons cornstarch
⅛ teaspoon salt
2¼ cups milk
2 squares (1 ounce each) unsweetened
  chocolate, melted
1½ teaspoons vanilla

In a medium saucepan, combine sugar, cornstarch and salt. Gradually stir in milk, whisking until smooth. Cook over medium heat, whisking constantly, until mixture boils. Boil 1 minute. Off heat, stir in melted chocolate and vanilla. Pour into individual serving dishes, cover and chill until cold. Makes 4 to 6 servings.

It is not known when this simple pudding originated, but it appeared regularly in cookbooks early in the century. A French name for "white food," blanc mange sometimes had chocolate added, a misnomer for sure. By mid-century, most recipes were simply called "pudding."

1900-1909 • FACTS • 1900-1909

Frankfurters became known as hot dogs after a sports cartoonist, using the common belief that Coney Island sausages contained dog meat, depicted a mustard-coated dachshund in a bun with the caption, "Get your hot dogs."

Perfection Salad won third prize in a recipe contest.

1900

Created by Auguste Escoffier in honor of opera singer Madame Nellie Melba in 1894, the dessert became known to the general public later. Escoffier's original was a poached peach half topped with vanilla ice cream and cardinale sauce – a puree of raspberries flavored with kirsch – and slivered almonds. Today's versions tend to be simpler, made with fresh or canned peaches and pureed raspberries.

Peach Melba

1 cup fresh or frozen unsweetened raspberries, thawed
¼ cup sugar
2 fresh peaches, peeled, halved and pitted or 4 canned peach halves, well-drained
4 scoops vanilla ice cream

Force raspberries through a fine sieve to extract the seeds. Place juice in a small saucepan with the sugar. Heat, stirring, until sugar is dissolved and mixture in slightly reduced. Chill.

Place peach halves, pit sides up, in individual dessert bowls. Top with a scoop of vanilla ice cream and ¼ of the raspberry sauce. Makes 4 servings.

1900-1909 • FACTS • 1900-1909

The federal Pure Food and Drug Act – the first law to protect America's food supply – went into effect.

❧

The first edition of The Settlement Cookbook was published.

1910 to 1919

The food Americans put on their tables from 1910 to 1919 was heavily influenced by World War I, increasing industrialization and a huge influx of immigrants.

World War I, from 1914 to 1918, brought food shortages and soaring prices so Americans planted gardens and developed new recipes for eggless-butterless cakes and meat-free main dishes.

Herbert Hoover, the U.S. Food Administrator, asked Americans to voluntarily observe wheatless Mondays and Wednesdays, meatless Tuesdays and porkless Thursdays and Saturdays. Victory bread made of soy flour was promoted by the Department of Agriculture, but production of soybeans was low and processing facilities were few.

Sugar was rationed in 1918, but Crisco arrived in time to pinch hit for hard-to-get lard.

Food prices, meanwhile, escalated. From 1914 to 1919, milk rose from 9 cents to 15 cents per quart, sirloin steak from 32 cents to 61 cents per pound and eggs from 34 cents to 62 cents per dozen.

Recipes became more standardized and more widely available. The canning industry began to thrive, offering unparalleled convenience. Processed foods got a strong start with such introductions as Hellmann's mayonnaise, Oreo cookies, hamburger buns and All-Bran.

Shopping also got easier and faster with the revolution of self-service grocery stores. Two opened independently in California in 1912. Piggly Wiggly became the first supermarket chain after it opened a self-service market in Memphis in 1916, offering some 600 different food items.

For housewives, combination stoves (gas with wood or coal) or gas-only stoves made cooking a lot easier, and the invention of an oven thermometer in 1915 made baking more precise. Gas and electric refrigerators also were becoming available but were too costly for the average household. Early in the decade, refrigerators were selling for $900, about the price of a car.

Americans flocked to the cities; for the first time, city dwellers outnumbered farmers. Restaurants, diners, automats and cafeterias opened to feed the growing population.

On one end of the scale was the elegant Arnaud's which opened in 1918 in New Orleans; on the other was Nathan's, a hot dog stand that opened in 1916 in Coney Island.

Everyone, seemingly, had a taste for candy. Despite the sugar shortages during the war, per capita consumption of candy rose from 5.6 pounds in 1914 to 13.5 pounds in 1919.

The decade also saw one of the nation's largest waves of immigration, mainly to the nation's large cities. In 1910 alone, more than a million immigrants from all parts of the globe arrived in America, bringing their food heritages with them.

Hungarian goulash, Italian spaghetti, Swedish meatballs and Irish stew were among dishes added to America's culinary pot.

Eggs Benedict

2 English muffins
Butter
4 slices Canadian bacon
4 poached eggs

Hollandaise Sauce

2 tablespoons lemon juice
¼ cup water
¼ teaspoon salt
3 egg yolks
½ cup (1 stick) butter

Hollandaise Sauce: In a small saucepan, whisk together lemon juice, water, salt and egg yolks. Place over very low heat and cook, whisking constantly, until bubbles begin to appear around the edges. Do not allow mixture to simmer. Whisk in butter, one pat at a time, until each is incorporated and sauce is thickened. Place saucepan over warm, not hot, water, while preparing muffins.

Split muffins, butter and toast them. Heat Canadian bacon in a skillet until heated and lightly browned. Place muffin halves on serving plates. Place a slice of bacon and a poached egg on top. Spoon Hollandaise over the top. Makes 4 servings.

Although this dish is thought to have been invented at the end of the 19th century, its classic form – with Canadian bacon, English muffins and Hollandaise sauce – dates to early in the 20th century. Some credit the Waldorf-Astoria; others say Delmonico's created it for Ms. LeGrand Benedict, a regular patron of the restaurant.

By 1912, Eggs Benedict was so well known that Underwood Deviled Ham used its own version of the recipe in advertising.

The news in recent years that raw eggs, used in the preparation of traditional Hollandaise sauce, could be harmful, dampened the popularity of this dish. But new methods, involving slight cooking of the eggs, have been developed to ensure safety. Also commercial Hollandaise mixes can be substituted; pasteurized eggs or egg substitutes also can be used instead of regular eggs.

Neapolitan Jell-o

1 package (4-serving size) lemon gelatin
1 package (4-serving size) strawberry
 or raspberry gelatin
Boiling water
Whipped cream or custard for garnish

This recipe, adapted from Jell-O, dates to 1916. It was deemed to be "American's Most Famous Dessert."

Dissolve lemon gelatin in 2 cups boiling water. Pour ⅔ of it into a mold. When it is set, whip the rest, pour it on and let it harden. Dissolve a package of red gelatin in 2 cups boiling water. When it is cold, put ⅔ of it, a spoonful at a time, on the lemon gelatin. For the fourth layer, whip the rest of the red gelatin and pour it on the hardened plain layer. Each layer must be hard before the others are added. Serve with whipped cream or custard. Makes about 8 servings.

Nathan Handwerker, who sold hot dogs at Coney Island for 5¢ each, countered rumors that the sausages contained low-quality meat by hiring college students to stand at his counter wearing white coats and stethoscopes. Soon the rumor spread that even doctors were eating Nathan's hot dogs.

Crab Louis

1 head Bibb or Boston lettuce
2 cups cooked fresh crab meat
  (Dungeness, lump or back fin),
  shells and cartilage removed
2 tomatoes, cut into quarters
2 hard-cooked eggs, peeled and quartered

Dressing
½ cup mayonnaise
2 tablespoons chili sauce
1 tablespoon finely chopped green onions
1 tablespoon finely chopped green pepper
1 teaspoon lemon juice

Combine Dressing ingredients and set aside. Remove leaves from lettuce and use them as beds on 2 salad plates. Crumble crab meat and place on top. Arrange tomatoes and eggs on the side. Spoon dressing on top. Makes 2 servings.

It is unknown who created this dish or which Louis it was named for. Solari's restaurant in San Francisco had it on the menu as early as 1911, but the Olympic Club in Seattle and the St. Francis Hotel in San Francisco also have been given credit for the salad's origin.

Although many variations exist, Crab Louis basically is lump crab meat with tomatoes and hard-cooked eggs over a bed of greens. Mayonnaise, doctored with chili sauce or ketchup and other ingredients, forms the dressing.

1910-1919
FACTS
1910-1919

Electric skillets, toasters and waffle irons were shown at the New York Electric Exhibition.

1910

This recipe was adapted from one that appeared in a booklet titled "Best War Time Recipes," published by the Royal Baking Powder Co. in 1918. It contained recipes that conserved eggs, butter, milk and wheat flour.

Corn Bread

1¾ cups cornmeal
¼ cup flour
4 teaspoons baking powder
1 tablespoon sugar
1 teaspoon salt
1½ cups milk
2 tablespoons vegetable shortening, melted

Mix cornmeal, flour, baking powder, sugar and salt thoroughly. Stir in milk and melted shortening; beat well and pour into well-greased 8- or 9-inch square baking pan and bake in 425° oven 20 to 25 minutes. Makes about 9 servings.

An actress entering New York's harbor posed for newspaper photographers, exposing a considerable amount of leg. The newspapers called it "cheesecake," thus coining a new usage for the word.

Duchess Potatoes

3 cups mashed potatoes
2 eggs, lightly beaten
2 tablespoons butter or margarine
Salt and pepper to taste
Dash of paprika

Beat potatoes, eggs, butter, salt and pepper until combined and smooth. Spoon or pipe potato mixture into mounds or rosettes onto a greased baking sheet. Sprinkle with paprika. Brown in a 425° oven. Makes 4 to 6 servings.

When this simple potato dish was created or how it got its name is unknown, but it began appearing in cookbooks around the second decade. A haute way to serve mashed potatoes, it was popular during the first half of the 20th century. The potatoes often were piped around planked meat or fish and then browned in the oven.

1910-1919 · FACTS · 1910-1919

The United States banned the sale of absinthe, a liqueur made from wormwood and promoted as a cure-all, after it was blamed for everything from gastrointestinal irritation and convulsions to loss of hearing.

America's sweet tooth was sated with the premiere of Life Savers, Clark Bars, Marshmallow Fluff and Moon Pies.

1910

Although Lobster Newburg was created by Delmonico's in the late 1800s, it was William Howard Taft's favorite recipe while he was president, 1909 to 1913. Early 20th century cookbooks were rife with recipes for the luxurious creamed dish.

Lobster Newburg

½ cup (1 stick) butter
6 tablespoons flour
½ teaspoon salt
1½ cups whole milk
1 cup heavy whipping cream
2 egg yolks, beaten
½ cup dry sherry or other dry white wine
2 cups cooked fresh, frozen or canned
  lobster meat

In medium saucepan, melt butter. Stir in flour and salt; cook, stirring, until mixture is bubbly. Slowly whisk in milk, whisking constantly, until mixture is smooth. Add cream and cook, stirring constantly, until mixture thickens and boils. Stir a little of the cream mixture into the egg yolks, whisking constantly. Return mixture to pan and bring back to a boil. Stir in sherry. Remove from heat and stir in lobster. Serve over toast points or in pastry shells. Makes about 6 servings.

Cookbook author and TV "French Chef" Julia Child was born in 1912.

꧁꧂

Fanny Farmer died in 1915.

Red Flannel Hash

½ pound cooked corned beef, diced
½ pound cooked cold potatoes, diced
½ cup diced onion
½ cup canned beets, drained and diced
1 tablespoon vegetable oil

Combine beef, potatoes, onion and beets. Heat oil in a medium skillet. Add beef mixture and cook until bottom is brown and crisp. Turn and brown other side. Add water if mixture seems dry. Makes about 4 servings.

Brining meat to preserve and flavor it remained popular even after fresh meat became readily available. This dish, which was especially popular in New England, was a good way to use up leftover corned beef. The name comes from the vibrant color the beets gave the hash.

1910·1919 · FACTS · 1910·1919

The American Dietetic Association was founded in 1917.

⟞⟟

President Woodrow Wilson ordered a 1,700-piece set of Lennox china for the White House.

1910

Chop Suey

1 pound lean pork steak or beef round steak
Flour
2 tablespoons shortening or vegetable oil
2 ribs celery, sliced
1 medium onion, chopped
1 cup sliced mushrooms
Salt and pepper
Cooked rice

Cut meat into thin strips and coat with flour. In a skillet, heat shortening and brown the meat. Add water to cover and simmer until meat is almost tender. Add celery, onion, mushrooms and seasonings. Cover and simmer until tender, about 30 minutes more. Stir occasionally to keep mixture from sticking. It should be thick like stew. Serve over rice. Makes about 4 servings.

Several stories exist about the origin of chop suey. Some say it was created by Chinese cooks to serve men who worked on the Pacific railroad in the middle of the 19th century. Others say it was first made in New York City by a cook serving a Chinese emissary. In the early part of the 20th century, supposedly it was served in Chinese restaurants that catered to American customers.

This dish, a mishmash of leftover meat and vegetables, is unlike the all-American chop suey enjoyed today, but it was the rage in the second decade.

Planter's Mr. Peanut was born.

———

Marcel Proust's remembrances in <u>Swann's Way</u> *made readers hungry for the butter cake called madeleine.*

Turkey Tetrazzini

¼ cup (½ stick) butter or margarine
¼ cup chopped onion
½ pound fresh mushrooms, sliced
3 tablespoons flour
1 cup chicken broth
1 cup light cream or half & half
¼ cup dry white wine
Salt and pepper to taste
½ cup Parmesan cheese
3 cups diced, cooked turkey or chicken
8 ounces spaghetti, cooked, drained

This dish was created for the Italian singer Luisa Tetrazzini, who toured the United States from 1910 to 1913. It was especially popular during the '50s with aspiring gourmets, who could make it with relative ease and impress their guests. Chicken is often used as a substitute for the turkey.

In a medium saucepan, melt butter. Add onion and mushrooms; cook, stirring, until tender. Stir in flour, cooking until bubbly, then add chicken broth and cream, stirring constantly, until thickened and bubbly. Stir in wine and seasonings. Remove from heat, stir in Parmesan cheese. Fold in turkey and spaghetti, blending well.

Transfer to a 3-quart baking dish and bake, uncovered, at 350° for about 20 to 25 minutes or until bubbly and lightly browned. Makes about 6 servings.

Kitchen cabinets, Pyrex baking dishes and KitchenAid standard mixers were introduced.

⬥⬥⬥

Crisco, corn oil and Campbell's cream of celery soup were introduced.

1910

War Cake

1 cup light corn syrup
1 cup water
1 cup raisins
2 tablespoons shortening or lard
1 teaspoon ground cinnamon
½ teaspoon ground cloves
½ teaspoon ground nutmeg
½ teaspoon salt
2 cups flour
1 teaspoon baking soda
½ teaspoon baking powder

Grease and flour an 8-by-4-inch loaf pan. In a medium saucepan, combine corn syrup, water, raisins, shortening, spices and salt. Bring to a boil and simmer gently 3 minutes. Let cool to room temperature.

Stir together the flour, baking soda and baking powder. Stir into liquid mixture, mixing just until combined. Pour into prepared pan and bake at 350° until a toothpick inserted into the center comes out clean, 45 to 55 minutes. Let cool in pan 10 minutes, then turn out onto a wire rack to cool completely.

1910-1919 • 1910-1919 • FACTS

Morton's poured out the first free-flowing salt and introduced the slogan, "When it rains, it pours."

The 5¢ Hershey bar was upsized from ⁹/₁₆ ounce to ¹⁵/₁₆ ounce.

1920 to 1929

The Roaring '20s did indeed roar despite a sober beginning and a crashing end.

Prohibition went into effect in January 1920, leading to the creation of cocktail parties and speak-easies. A majority of the cocktails that Americans drink today were created during this period, when home parties, featuring alcoholic drinks and tidbits of food, were the rage.

Scores of restaurants that had relied on liquor sales closed their doors. Among them was New York City's venerable Delmonico's, ending a 92-year run. Replacing these restaurants were speak-easies, which served food as well as illegal drinks.

Tea rooms and cafeterias blossomed, as well as roadside diners, thanks to the growing auto industry. But the best food was still served in hotel dining rooms.

The ban on liquor fostered a new appetite for soft drinks, ice cream sodas and coffee. Candy sales also thrived, partly because sweets counteracted the bitterness of bootlegged alcohol.

The stock market was booming and the well-to-do were eating lobster Newburg, artichokes with Hollandaise and chocolate éclairs. On the home front, dinner tables were filled with meat, poultry, fish and vegetables.

Housewives could afford the laborsaving devices entering the market. Sales of refrigerators jumped from 10,000 in 1920 to 800,000 in 1929, thanks to the low average price of $292. Gas ranges replaced wood and coal stoves. Pop-up toasters and stainless steel knives were among the new products offered.

Convenience food also began to bud. Quick-cooking rolled oats, pancake mix and canned goods (everything from tuna to pineapple) were available. By the end of the decade, families could buy pre-sliced bread, canned baby food and Velveeta.

Sales of Jell-O, which had been on the market since the late 1800s, exploded, as refrigerators made chilling food much easier.

By 1929, Clarence Birdseye had developed a technique to quick-freeze vegetables, heralding the dawn of the frozen-food industry.

While convenience foods and kitchen appliances seemingly saved time in the kitchen, many middle-class women joined the labor force, giving them less time for household duties. Furthermore, by this time, domestic help was mainly a memory.

At least there was more cooking and housekeeping advice available. Scientists were discovering vitamins, and home economists were busy developing recipes and menus to ensure the economic and physical well-being of families.

Radio programs, food- and appliance-company pamphlets and cookbooks, such as <u>Mrs. Allen on Cooking, Menus, Service: 2,500 Recipes</u> by Ida C. Bailey Allen, provided plenty of ideas for home cooks.

The so-called "Jazz Age" of the '20s, with its high-flying lifestyle, came to a halt in October 1929 when the stock market crashed.

Carrot Pineapple Salad

1 can (8 ounces) crushed pineapple
2 tablespoons lemon juice
Cold water
1 package (4-serving size) lemon gelatin
1 cup boiling water
¾ cup grated carrots

As home sales of refrigerators thrived, so did gelatin salads. This was one of the popular ones.

Drain pineapple, reserving the juices. To the juices, add lemon juice and enough water to make 1 cup. Dissolve gelatin in boiling water. Stir in juice mixture. Chill until mixture begins to set. Stir in crushed pineapple and grated carrots. Chill until set. Makes about 6 servings.

1920-1929 · FACTS · 1920-1929

Store-sliced bread, more convenient and generally thinner than home-sliced, led to increased use of butter, jam, peanut butter and cheese.

Caesar Salad

1 clove garlic
1 head romaine lettuce
⅓ cup olive oil
1 coddled egg, optional, see note below
3 tablespoons lemon juice
¼ teaspoon salt
⅛ teaspoon pepper
¼ cup freshly grated Parmesan cheese
2 cups crisp croutons

Created by Alex Cardini in Tijuana, Mexico, in 1924, this salad was a makeshift combination of the sparse ingredients he found in his brother's restaurant. Cardini, an Italian Air Force veteran, originally named the salad Aviator Salad. Later he changed it to Caesar, his brother's name. Anchovies, a part of today's classic salad, were added later.

Cut garlic clove in half and rub the cut sides against the inside of the salad bowl. Discard the garlic. Tear lettuce leaves into bite-sized pieces into the salad bowl. Drizzle with olive oil. Break egg, if using, into the salad bowl. Combine lemon juice, salt and pepper; drizzle the mixture over the egg and greens. Toss to coat all the greens. Sprinkle cheese on top and mix lightly. Top with croutons. Makes about 6 servings.

Note: A coddled egg is one that has been soft-cooked for 1 minute. Because of the danger of consuming raw or undercooked eggs, use a pasteurized egg or substitute ¼ cup refrigerated or frozen and thawed egg product. If preferred, the egg can be omitted.

1920-1929
• FACTS •
1920-1929

Lindy's and Sardi's restaurants opened their doors in New York City.

Cobb Salad

1 small head iceberg lettuce
1 small head romaine lettuce
2 cups poached or roasted chicken
 breast meat, diced
2 tomatoes, chopped
2 hard-cooked eggs, finely chopped
1 avocado, peeled, pitted and diced
6 strips bacon, cooked and crumbled
½ cup crumbled Roquefort cheese
Bottled French dressing

Robert Cobb, owner of The Brown Derby restaurant, invented this decorative salad. Today's classic version is nearly the same as the original, with one exception: Cobb supposedly stopped on his way to work to buy watercress for the salad. Modern recipes use iceberg lettuce and sometimes romaine instead.

Tear lettuces into bite-sized pieces. Divide among individual shallow salad or soup bowls. Neatly arrange chicken, tomatoes, eggs, avocado, bacon and cheese, in separate sections, either spoke fashion or in a striped pattern. Serve with dressing on the side. Makes about 4 servings.

The boysenberry, a cross between blackberries, raspberries and loganberries, was developed by Rudolph Boysen, a U.S. breeder.

Betty Crocker was born in 1921.

1920

Recipes for this super-sweet side dish began appearing in cookbooks in the 1920s.

Sweet Potatoes with Marshmallow Topping

4 medium-sized sweet potatoes
¼ cup (½ stick) butter or margarine
¼ cup firmly packed brown sugar
¼ cup milk
Dash of ground cinnamon, optional
Marshmallows

Boil potatoes with skins on until tender. Drain and peel. While potatoes are still hot, mash with an electric mixer until smooth. Add butter, brown sugar, milk and cinnamon, if desired. Beat until combined. Place in a greased baking dish. Cover the top with marshmallows. Place in a 350° oven and bake until mixture is hot and marshmallows are browned, about 30 minutes. Makes 4 to 6 servings.

Heart disease became the leading cause of death, overtaking tuberculosis.

❧

General Mills and General Foods were organized.

Date-Nut Loaf

1½ cups water
1½ cups pitted, chopped dates
½ cup sugar
2 tablespoons vegetable shortening
1 egg
2¼ cups flour
1 teaspoon baking soda
½ teaspoon salt
½ teaspoon ground cinnamon
1 cup coarsely chopped walnuts

Baking powder-leavened breads date to the mid 1800s, but nut loaves similar to those found today, began appearing in the 1920s when baking powders became more dependable. Modern recipes are more apt to call for baking soda, as does this one.

Bring water to a boil and pour over the dates. Let stand until cool. In a mixing bowl, beat together the sugar and shortening until light and fluffy. Beat in egg. Add date-water mixture. Mix the flour, soda, salt and cinnamon. Stir into mixing bowl, blending just until combined. Fold in nuts.

Pour into a well-greased 9-by-5-inch loaf pan and bake at 350° for about 1 hour or until a wooden pick inserted into the center comes out clean. Let bread stand 15 minutes, then remove from the pan to a wire rack to cool completely.

1920-1929 • FACTS • 1920-1929

Botulism deaths brought new safety standards for the canning industry.

⸎

Eskimo Pie, Wise potato chips and White Castle hamburgers made their debut.

1920

*Swiss steak in the '20s
was little more than
round steak, floured
and browned, then
simmered in water
until tender. Tomatoes,
onions and other
ingredients were later
additions.*

Swiss Steak

2 pound beef round steak, 1-inch thick
½ cup flour
¾ teaspoon salt
¼ teaspoon pepper
2 tablespoons vegetable shortening
1½ cups water
1 medium onion, chopped
1 can (14½ ounces) tomatoes, undrained

Trim fat and bones from steak. Combine
flour, salt and pepper. Pound flour mixture
into the steak using a meat mallet or the edge
of a sturdy plate. Heat shortening in a skillet
until hot. Add steak and cook until browned
on both sides. Add water, cover and cook over
medium-low heat, about 1 hour. Add onion
and tomatoes; continue cooking until meat is
tender, about 1 hour more. Makes 4 to
6 servings.

*Candy sales thrived. New "sweet"
introductions included Baby
Ruth, Mounds, Oh Henry!, Reese's
Peanut Butter Cup, Bit-O-Honey,
Dum Dum suckers, Milk Duds
and Butterfinger.*

Fettucine Alfredo

8 ounces fettuccine
⅓ cup butter
⅓ cup freshly grated Parmesan cheese
Freshly ground black pepper

Cook fettuccine in boiling salted water according to package directions. Drain. Cut butter into pieces and place in serving bowl. Add hot pasta and cheese. Toss thoroughly until pasta is coated with melted butter and cheese. Add pepper to taste. Makes 2 to 3 servings.

Alfredo Di Lelio is credited with inventing this rich dish at his restaurant in Rome. Douglas Fairbanks and Mary Pickford were so enchanted they ate it almost daily while on their honeymoon in 1927. Its popularity spread, but it would take several decades before the butter-laced pasta was adopted by home cooks.

A Nebraska inventor named Edwin E. Perkins took his Fruit Smack soft drink concentrate, sold in heavy breakable bottles, to a chemist to reduce the concentrate to a dry powder. Perkins named the new product Kool-Aid.

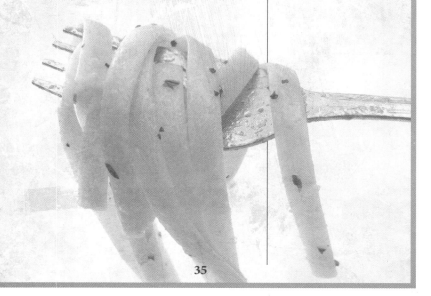

1920

Spaghetti with Meat Sauce

Immigrants from southern Italy introduced Americans to a new way of serving macaroni and spaghetti – with tomato sauce. Early cookbook recipes, usually titled Italian spaghetti, were made with canned or fresh tomatoes thickened with flour. Sometimes grated cheese, onion and green peppers were added. Meat was introduced to the mix, probably during Prohibition, when Italian-American restaurant owners took advantage of the abundant supply to please their American customers.

1 pound ground beef
1 onion, chopped
½ cup chopped green pepper
1 clove garlic, minced
2 cans (14½ ounces each) tomatoes, undrained
½ teaspoon salt
⅛ teaspoon pepper
1 pound spaghetti
Parmesan cheese, optional

Brown ground beef with the onion, green pepper and garlic. Drain off drippings. Add tomatoes, breaking them into pieces. Season with salt and pepper. Simmer, covered, over low heat until sauce has thickened, about 30 minutes. Stir occasionally.

Meanwhile, cook spaghetti in boiling salted water according to package directions. Drain. Place on individual plates and top with sauce. Sprinkle with Parmesan cheese, if desired. Makes 4 to 6 servings.

Within a four-month period in 1920, the price of sugar dropped from 30¢ a pound to 8¢ a pound.

Wonder Bread arrived.

Heavenly Hash

1 can (8¾ ounces) pineapple chunks,
  drained
½ cup maraschino cherries, well drained
½ cup chopped walnuts
1½ cups miniature marshmallows
2 cups cooked rice, cooled
1 cup whipping cream
2 tablespoons sugar

Stir pineapple, cherries, walnuts and
marshmallows into the rice. Whip cream,
slowly adding the sugar, until stiff peaks form.
Fold into rice mixture. Chill. Makes about
6 servings.

*Tea rooms and ladies'
luncheons in the
'20s featured dainty
sandwiches, fruit
salads and fluffy,
super-sweet desserts.
Typical of the time was
this rice dessert.*

*The newly introduced broccoli was
scorned in a* New Yorker *cartoon
showing a child refusing to eat the
vegetable. The caption,
by E. B. White, read, "I say it's
spinach and I say the hell with it."*

*Hershey's nickel candy bar grew
from 1 ounce to 1⅜ ounces due
to lower cocoa prices.*

1920

Imagine making this frosting with a rotary mixer, as was used when this classic recipe first appeared in the late '20s. To make it, egg whites, water and sugar are beaten over boiling water for seven minutes until fluffy. Hand-held electric mixers make the job easier and take less time.

Seven-Minute Icing

2 egg whites
1½ cups sugar
¼ teaspoon cream of tartar
⅓ cup cold water
1½ teaspoons vanilla

Place egg whites, sugar, cream of tartar and water in top of a double boiler. Place over gently simmering water and beat with a mixer until mixture holds stiff peaks, 4 to 7 minutes. Fold in vanilla.

1920-1929 · FACTS · 1920-1929

California realtor Bill Hamlin developed a formula for a smooth, frothy orange drink, which was sold at Julius Freed's fresh orange juice stand. Customers liked it so much that Freed's sales increased from $20 to $100 a day. "Give me an orange, Julius," customers ordered. Hamlin quit the real estate business and by the end of the decade had 100 Orange Julius stands grossing nearly $3 million.

Pineapple Upside-Down Cake

6 tablespoons butter or margarine
1 cup firmly packed brown sugar
7 slices canned pineapple
Maraschino cherries and pecan halves
¼ cup vegetable shortening
1 cup sugar
2 eggs
1½ cups flour
1½ teaspoons baking powder
½ teaspoon salt
½ cup milk
1 teaspoon vanilla

This cake, most sources agree, originated in the '20s. Exactly when and by whom, is not so clear. Some say the recipe, then-titled Pineapple Glace, was printed in a fund-raising cookbook in Seattle in 1924. Others report that when the Hawaiian Pineapple Co. – the predecessor of Dole Food Co. – held a recipe contest in 1925, 2,500 of the 60,000 entries were for pineapple upside-down cake. Still another source said the upside-down cake was the winner of the contest.

Melt butter in a heavy 10-inch skillet. Stir in brown sugar and simmer until sugar melts. Remove from heat and arrange the pineapple slices in the skillet. Place cherries and pecans in the center of each slice. Set aside.

Heat oven to 350°. In mixer, beat shortening and granulated sugar until light and fluffy. Beat in eggs, one at a time, until combined. Combine flour, baking powder and salt; add to shortening mixture alternately with the milk, beginning and ending with the flour mixture. Stir in vanilla.

Pour batter over the pineapple in the skillet and bake 35 to 45 minutes or until a wooden pick inserted into the center comes out clean. Cool cake 15 minutes, then invert onto a round serving plate. Serve warm or at room temperature. Top with whipped cream, if desired. Makes 8 to 10 servings.

1920

Strawberry Chiffon Pie

Light and airy chiffon pies began appearing in cookbooks around the '20s. Made with eggs, gelatin and sometimes whipped cream, they were flavored with fruits, chocolate, eggnog or pumpkin. They were chilled, rather than baked. When raw eggs became suspect in the '80s, chiffon pies lost much of their favor. Current recipes use pasteurized or powdered egg whites or have been reformulated to eliminate the egg whites. This one uses pasteurized eggs.

1 pint fresh strawberries
⅔ cup sugar
1 envelope unflavored gelatin
½ cup cold water
3 pasteurized egg whites
¼ teaspoon cream of tartar
⅓ cup sugar
½ cup whipping cream, whipped
1 9-inch baked pie shell

Hull and finely crush strawberries. Stir in ⅔ cup sugar and set aside until sugar is dissolved. Soften gelatin in cold water. Heat, stirring, until gelatin is dissolved. Stir into strawberry mixture and chill until partially set.

Beat egg whites with cream of tartar until fluffy. Slowly beat in ⅓ cup sugar and beat until stiff peaks are formed. Fold into strawberry mixture. Fold in whipped cream. Turn into prepared pie shell and refrigerate until set.

If desired, serve topped with additional whipped cream. Garnish, if desired, with sliced fresh strawberries.

1920-1929
· FACTS ·
1920-1929

Cobb Salad was created at The Brown Derby restaurant in Los Angeles by the owner Robert Cobb.

1930 to 1939

Times were bitter in the '30s following the stock market crash. Unemployment in the United States reached nearly 17 million in 1932, leading to bread lines and soup kitchens, even fistfights over garbage.

Americans lucky enough to have work were averaging around $17 per week. For the unlucky, relief checks for a family of five in New York were a mere $6 a week.

Cooks learned to stretch the pocketbook with meat extenders or meatless main dishes. Chili, macaroni and cheese, toasted cheese sandwiches, soup and creamed meat and vegetables on toast were common money-savers. Meat loaves were stretched to the hilt with bread crumbs or oats. Casseroles with beans and inexpensive vegetables, such as potatoes, peas and carrots, were popular meat substitutes or stretchers.

Despite the hard times, life in America had some sweet notes. Families continued to entertain, albeit casually at home.

Welsh rabbit and creamed chipped beef over waffles replaced caviar and veal cutlets on company menus. One-dish suppers, potluck buffets, parties with refreshments rather than meals and church socials were important ways to socialize.

Afternoon teas and club luncheons offered hostesses a chance to be creative, even glamorous. Bite-sized sandwiches, cut into decorative shapes, were filled with deviled ham and pickle relish or cream cheese and fruit. Dainty cookies and petits fours were put on *the table to impress.*

Creamed chicken in patty shells, timbales, heart-shaped molded salads and meringue torte also were in vogue.

Decoration was of utmost importance. Radish and tomato roses, sugar cubes painted with flowers, topiary salads and citrus baskets added panache to plates. The crowning glory of the club luncheon was the sandwich loaf, made with several fillings, then "frosted" to look like a cake.

Industry continued to roll out electric appliances for housewives during the '30s. Chafing dishes, coffeemakers, waffle irons and hot plates were among the popular items. Pressure cookers also made their debut. But probably the most versatile kitchen helper of the time was the electric roaster. It was a large portable oven that could serve as a turkey roaster, picnic basket, fish broiler or a meal-maker for a crowd.

Prohibition was repealed at the end of 1933, leading to the re-emergence of restaurants and bars. The Rainbow Room in New York City, the Pump Room in Chicago and the London Chop House in Detroit opened in the '30s, the last offering 75-cent steak dinners and 25-cent scotch and sodas. Sales of soft drink and ice cream sodas took a hit when liquor became available, but 7-Up, which was promoted as a mixer, increased dramatically in sales.

By the end of the decade, the number of unemployed had dropped to 9.5 million, but wages were still low and war was threatening. No wonder the era was called The Great Depression.

Ginger Ale Salad

2 packages (4-serving size) lemon gelatin
2 cups boiling water
2 cups ginger ale or 7-Up
1 can (20 ounces) crushed pineapple
2 bananas, sliced
1 cup miniature marshmallows
½ cup sugar
2 tablespoons flour
1 egg, beaten
2 tablespoons butter or margarine
1 cup whipped cream or frozen
 whipped topping, thawed

The idea of putting soda pop in a congealed salad probably started early in the century, but by this period it was well-established and well-loved. Early recipes called for crystallized ginger in addition to the soft drink; later recipes were made with 7-Up. This is a modern recipe in which either ginger ale or 7-Up can be used.

 Dissolve gelatin in boiling water. Add ginger ale and chill until thick, but not firm. Drain pineapple, reserving liquid. Fold pineapple, bananas and marshmallows into gelatin. Chill until firm.
 For topping: Combine sugar, flour and reserved pineapple juice. Heat over medium heat, stirring, until mixture boils. Pour a little of the mixture into the beaten egg, beating constantly. Return mixture to pan and heat until mixture thickens and begins to bubble. Remove from heat and stir in butter. Let cool, then fold in whipped cream.
 Cut gelatin into squares and serve with a dollop of topping. Makes about 8 servings.

Joy of Cooking made its first public appearance. It was written by a 60-year-old St. Louis housewife, Irma Rombauer, whose lawyer husband taught her to cook.

1930-1939 · FACTS · 1930-1939

Sandwich Loaf

1 unsliced loaf of white sandwich bread
¼ cup (½ stick) butter or margarine,
  softened

First layer
4 ounces store-bought pimento cheese
Milk or cream

Second layer
3 hard-cooked eggs, finely chopped
2 tablespoons mayonnaise

Third layer
1 package (3 ounces) cream cheese, softened
½ cucumber, peeled, seeded and grated
6 sprigs parsley, finely minced

Fourth layer
½ cup store-bought ham salad

Frosting:
1 package (8 ounces) cream cheese, softened
Milk or cream
Garnishes: sliced stuffed olives, toasted
  almonds, pimento strips, parsley sprigs,
  radish roses

The ultimate treat at bridal showers and women's club luncheons, frosted bread loaves with colorful fillings could inspire oohs and aahs from party guests. Although rather time-consuming to make, the loaves could be prepared well in advance and kept safely in the refrigerator until guests arrived.

Remove crust from bread. Slice loaf horizontally into 5 even layers. Spread each slice with butter. Mix pimento cheese with enough milk or cream to make it spreadable. Spread on bottom layer, then top with a second layer of bread. Combine hard-cooked eggs and mayonnaise and spread on second layer.

Top with another slice of bread. Combine cream cheese, cucumber and parsley. Spread on bread.

Top with another slice of bread and spread with ham salad. Top with final slice of bread. Mix cream cheese with enough milk or cream to make it spreadable. Frost top and sides of loaf with mixture. Decorate as desired using any of the suggested garnishes.

Cover with plastic wrap and chill at least 2 hours. To serve, cut crosswise into 1-inch slices. Makes 12 to 14 servings.

Cioppino

¼ cup olive oil

5 cloves garlic, minced

1 cup chopped onion

1 cup chopped celery

1 cup chopped green pepper

1 can (14½ ounces) Italian tomatoes, chopped

1 can (15 ounces) tomato sauce

1 bottle (8 ounces) clam juice

1 cup water

2 cups dry white wine

1 bay leaf

½ teaspoon oregano

½ teaspoon basil

1 teaspoon salt, or to taste

½ teaspoon black pepper

1 pound fresh or frozen firm white fish, such as cod, cut into chunks

1 pound shrimp, peeled and deveined

1 can (6½ ounces) crab meat

1 can (10 ounces) whole clams

¼ cup minced fresh parsley

The date of origin for this fish stew is undetermined, but San Francisco is generally credited as the place of birth. It was popularized in the '30s. Although the dish became known throughout the United States after World War II, it remains closely tied to the West Coast even today. This version is simplified for use where fresh seafood may not be readily available.

In large kettle, heat olive oil. Add garlic, onion, celery and green pepper; sauté, stirring occasionally, until softened. Add tomatoes, tomato sauce, clam juice, water, wine and seasonings. Cover and simmer 30 minutes. Add white fish and shrimp; cook about 20 minutes. Add crab meat and clams; heat through. Sprinkle with parsley. Makes about 6 servings.

1930-1939 FACTS 1930-1939

The size of the nickel Hershey Bar changed at least five times from 1930 to 1938. It ended the same size it started, at 1⅜ ounces.

1930

Chili

1 pound coarsely ground beef chuck
1 medium onion, chopped
1 clove garlic, minced
1 can (14½ ounces) chopped tomatoes
1 cup water
½ teaspoon salt
1 tablespoon chili powder
½ teaspoon ground cumin
1 can (15 ounces) kidney or pinto beans,
  undrained

In a heavy saucepan, sauté beef, onion and garlic until beef is no longer pink. Drain off drippings. Add remaining ingredients, cover and simmer until flavors have melded and mixture has thickened slightly. Stir occasionally. Makes about 4 servings.

Chili probably is as old as the hills, but "bowls of red" as known today date more closely to the '20s and '30s. Of course, no one agrees on what chili really is. Ground beef, or chunks of beef, or no meat at all? Beans and tomatoes? Chili powder or dried chilies? It depends on whom you ask. Whatever the recipe, chili was a popular Sunday night supper during the Depression. This recipe takes the middle ground.

Sweet tooths could indulge in Heath Bar, 3 Musketeers, Kit Kat and Snickers for the first time.

∞

The Waldorf-Astoria opened on Park Avenue in New York with its own butcher shop, bakery and ice plant. The maître d'hôtel, hired from the old Waldorf, earned $30,000 a year. At the time, doctors were earning about $5,000 and farm hands only $216 per year.

Porcupine Meat Balls

1½ pounds ground beef
½ cup uncooked long-grain rice
¼ cup finely chopped onion
1 teaspoon salt
⅛ teaspoon black pepper
1 can (10½ ounces) tomato soup
1 soup can water

Combine ground beef, rice, onion, salt and pepper. Form into 1-inch balls. Combine soup and water in a large, heavy saucepan. Bring to a simmer. Add meatballs, cover and simmer gently 1 hour. Makes about 6 servings.

Porcupine meatballs, or rice meatballs, were popular in the '30s as a means of stretching meat. One early recipe called for a pound of chopped beef and "3 handfuls rice" which were formed into balls and cooked in water for one and a half hours. A can of tomato soup was added in the end, then the meatballs were served over mashed potatoes. This is a more modern recipe.

The Harry & David mail-order fruit business premiered.

⌒⌒⌒

Instead of sending Christmas cards, Duncan Hines, a Chicago printing salesman, sent a pamphlet listing his favorite eating places. He received so many requests for copies, he started a business leasing "Recommended by Duncan Hines" signs for some $20 a year.

1930

Meatless Meat Loaf

When times were tough, inventive housewives could make a main dish "loaf" from almost anything. This recipe, adapted from 1938 edition of The Home Dietitian's Cook Book, *relied on nuts.*

2 cups broken pecan meats or mixed nuts
2 cups dry whole-wheat bread crumbs
1 cup chopped celery
¼ cup chopped onion
1 teaspoon celery salt
½ teaspoon paprika
½ teaspoon dry mustard
2 eggs, beaten
Cream or milk
2 tablespoons butter or margarine
½ cup hot water

Put nuts, crumbs, celery and onion through a food chopper; add seasonings and mix well. Add eggs and enough cream or milk to moisten so the mixture will form a loaf in a shallow pan or casserole. Bake at 350° for 1½ hours. Combine butter and water; use to baste loaf occasionally as it bakes. Serve hot or cold. Makes 4 to 6 servings.

1930-1939 FACTS

A flour salesman boarded a train late one evening and was so impressed with the biscuits he was served that he asked the chef how they were made. After learning the chef kept a mixture of flour, lard, baking powder and salt in the icebox for late orders, the salesman approached his company with the idea. Thus, Bisquick was born.

Chicken Divan

4 skinless, boneless chicken breast halves
1 stalk (about 10 ounces) fresh broccoli
¼ cup (½ stick) butter or margarine
5 tablespoons flour
2 cups milk
¼ cup dry white wine
1 egg yolk, lightly beaten
Salt and white pepper to taste
½ cup Parmesan cheese

This dish was created in the '30s at the Divan Parisien restaurant in New York City. The restaurant is gone, but the recipe is still popular today.

Poach chicken breasts in water to cover just until no longer pink inside. Remove from water. When cool enough to handle, slice breasts in half horizontally. Set aside.

Trim leaves and woody ends from broccoli. Cut broccoli lengthwise into stems. Cook in boiling water until almost tender. Drain.

In a medium saucepan, melt butter. Stir in flour until smooth, then add milk, whisking constantly. Cook, stirring, until mixture thickens and boils. Stir in wine. Pour a little of the sauce into the beaten yolk, whisking to blend. Return all of mixture to the saucepan and bring back to a boil. Stir in seasoning and Parmesan cheese. Remove from heat.

Place broccoli stems in one layer in a shallow baking pan. Place chicken breast slices on top. Pour sauce over the chicken, covering completely.

Bake, uncovered, in a 350° oven 20 to 30 minutes or until bubbly and lightly browned. Makes about 6 servings.

The Better Homes and Gardens Cookbook *premiered.* *Within the following 45 years, some 15 million copies were sold, making it the all-time best-selling U.S. cookbook.*

1930

Tuna Noodle Casserole

1 can (10¾ ounces) cream
 of mushroom soup
½ cup milk
2 cups hot cooked noodles, drained
1 cup cooked peas, drained
2 tablespoons chopped pimento,
 drained, optional
2 cans (6 ounces each) tuna, drained
2 tablespoons dry bread crumbs
1 tablespoon butter or margarine, melted

Mix soup, milk, noodles, peas, pimentos if desired and tuna. Turn into a greased 1½-quart casserole. Bake, uncovered, at 400° for 20 minutes. Mix crumbs and butter. Sprinkle over tuna and bake 5 minutes or until browned. Makes about 4 servings.

White Castle, which was selling its burgers for five cents each, advertised a five-for-a-dime promotion for one day, from 2 p.m. to midnight. Crowds lined up before the starting time and by 3 p.m., most of the stands had run out of meat and buns. Supply houses called their employees back to work to fill the demand.

Toll House Cookies

2¼ cups flour
1 teaspoon baking soda
1 teaspoon salt
1 cup (2 sticks) butter or margarine, softened
¾ cup sugar
¾ cup firmly packed brown sugar
1 teaspoon vanilla
2 eggs
1 package (12 ounces) semi-sweet chocolate chips

Combine flour, soda and salt. In a mixing bowl, cream butter, sugars and vanilla until light and fluffy. Add eggs, one at a time, beating well after each addition. Gradually beat in flour mixture, mixing just until combined. By hand, stir in chocolate chips.

Drop by rounded tablespoonfuls onto ungreased baking sheets 2 inches apart. Bake at 375° for 9 to 11 minutes or until golden brown. Cool on baking sheets for 2 minutes, then transfer to wire racks to cool completely. Makes about 5 dozen cookies.

Ruth Wakefield of Whitman, MA, created this recipe in 1933. She thought she would save the time it takes to melt chocolate by adding bits of semi-sweet chocolate to her cookie batter. She was surprised to discover the chocolate bits didn't melt in the oven as she'd hoped. The recipe is named after the Toll House Inn that she and her husband owned. The Nestlé Corp. started selling chocolate chips in 1939 and bought the rights to the Toll House name. Today chocolate chip cookies account for more than half of the cookies baked.

Typical food prices in 1933 were: rib roast, 22¢ per pound; potatoes, 2¢ per pound; sugar, 6¢ per pound; and eggs, 29¢ per dozen.

1930

Chocolate Applesauce Cake

Applesauce cakes were most popular during the '20s and '30s but may have had their origins during World War I. Early recipes often were made without eggs and with little sugar or shortening. This eggless recipe is baked in a cast-iron skillet. It is best served warm with just a sprinkle of confectioners' sugar or a dollop of whipped cream on top.

1 cup sugar
½ cup (1 stick) butter or margarine, softened
1½ cups applesauce
2 cups flour
1 tablespoon cornstarch
3 tablespoons cocoa
2 teaspoons baking soda
1 teaspoon ground cinnamon
½ teaspoon ground cloves
½ teaspoon ground nutmeg
1 cup raisins
1 cup chopped nuts

Grease and flour a 10-inch cast-iron skillet. Cream sugar and butter with a mixer until light and fluffy. Mix in applesauce. Combine dry ingredients and mix into applesauce mixture just until combined. Stir in raisins and nuts. Pour into prepared skillet and bake at 325° about 35 minutes or until a toothpick inserted into the center comes out clean.

The Waring Blender, with the backing of bandleader Fred Waring, was introduced at the National Restaurant Show in 1937.

Spam, Kraft Macaroni & Cheese Dinner, Ragú Spaghetti Sauce and Miracle Whip were born.

1940 to 1949

The cuisine of the 1940s can be divided in two – war years and postwar years – because the foods Americans ate during those periods were as different as hog jowls and pork roast.

By the time the United States entered World War II in 1941, consumers already were feeling the pinch on imported foods. Sage, thyme and coconut were scarce, and olive oil was priced at $9 to $11 a gallon.

But rationing, which began in 1942, had the most profound effect. Sales of sugar, coffee, canned goods, meat, fish, butter and cheese were limited according to a complicated points system, and home cooks were forced to make do.

Americans didn't starve though. In fact, per capita consumption of food was higher during the war than ever, but people were limited as to the foods they knew and loved.

Honey, corn syrup and molasses filled in for rationed sugar. Vegetable oils and margarine substituted for butter and olive oil.

Game (if ammunition was available), poultry, fish and offal were suggested as alternatives to beef and pork. Cookbooks featured dishes such as tripe casserole and hog jowls with turnip greens.

Ground beef, which required fewer rationing points than steaks or roasts, was extended by using it in spaghetti, meat rolls, stuffed peppers and meat loaves.

Victory gardens, considered a patriotic duty, were planted by the millions, accounting for as much as 40 percent of the total U.S.

vegetable production. Housewives saved tin cans and kitchen fat to help the war effort.

Interest in nutrition was high in the '40s. The government issued the Recommended Daily Allowances in 1941, but housewives had trouble relating the numbers to the foods they put on the table. The Basic Seven Food Groups, illustrated in a pie chart, was issued a year later to make "balanced" meal planning easier. Added to the challenges created by rationing, food shortages and strapped budgets, however, planning nutritious meals was hardly a snap.

Dehydrated food got a big boost during the war because it was lightweight and easy to ship to servicemen overseas. American housewives, too, endorsed dried soups, puddings and potato flakes. But industry went overboard, developing everything from clam powder to dried spinach and tomato juice. Cooks weren't impressed and the hoped-for boom was a bust.

The end of the war in 1945 brought big menu changes. Gardens were forgotten because cooks again could buy canned and frozen fruits and vegetables. Milk, cream, cheese and eggs were devoured.

But mostly, Americans wanted meat. Forget nut loaves and boiled tongue. Bring on the steaks, chops and roasts.

Women who came home after working in factories during the war no longer wanted to be slaves to the kitchen. They adopted convenience foods as they entered the market and bought the latest appliances as factories revved to full tilt.

Americans had money and unbridled optimism. They began to travel and to frequent continental-cuisine restaurants. This sparked an interest in foreign foods and gourmet cooking.

Bouillabaisse, beef Stroganoff, lobster Thermidor, crêpes suzette and strawberries Romanoff were considered haute cuisine, but within the realm of accomplished cooks.

Corn Pudding

2 cups canned whole-kernel corn,
well drained

3 eggs, well beaten

2 tablespoons butter or margarine, melted

2 teaspoons sugar

½ teaspoon salt

2 cups milk

Vegetables were served simply and nearly always overcooked in the '40s. "Fancy" or company vegetable dishes were creamed, scalloped or stuffed. Corn pudding was a classic of the era.

Combine all ingredients and place in a well-greased 1½-quart casserole. Place casserole in a larger pan and put 1 inch of boiling water in the larger pan. Bake at 350° for 30 to 40 minutes or until a knife inserted into the center comes out clean. Makes 4 to 6 servings.

Restaurant openings during the decade included Toots Shor's in New York, Brennan's in New Orleans and Arthur Bryant's Bar-B-Cue in Kansas City.

A 29-year-old entrepreneur and a short-order cook launched Mrs. Paul's Kitchens. Each invested $450 in a company that would market six-ounce packages of frozen deviled crabs for 59¢.

1940

Broiled Chicken Deluxe

2 3-pound broiler-fryers, each cut into quarters
Juice from 1 large lemon
4 teaspoons sugar
2 teaspoons salt
1 teaspoon paprika
½ teaspoon pepper
4 tablespoons butter or margarine, cut into small pieces

Place chicken skin-side up in broiling pan without rack. Pour lemon juice over chicken; sprinkle with sugar, salt, paprika and pepper. Turn chicken skin-side down; dot with butter.

Place broiling pan about 7 to 9 inches from heat source and broil chicken 25 minutes (or bake in 450° oven), basting chicken with butter as soon as butter melts.

Turn chicken skin-side up; brush with pan drippings. Broil 15 to 20 minutes, until juices run clear when chicken is pierced with a fork, brushing often with pan drippings.

Arrange chicken on a large warm platter. Skim fat from pan drippings; pour pan juices over chicken. Makes 8 servings.

1940·1949
FACTS
1940·1949

Gourmet *magazine premiered.*

No-Knead Water-Rising Twists

1940

2½ to 3½ cups flour, divided
1 cup sugar, divided
1 teaspoon salt
1 package active dry yeast
¾ cup milk
½ cup (1 stick) butter or margarine
1 teaspoon vanilla
2 eggs
½ cup chopped nuts
1 teaspoon ground cinnamon

This recipe won the first Pillsbury Bake-Off Contest in 1949. Theodora Smafield of Rockford, IL, walked off with $50,000. The recipe has been updated by Pillsbury.

In a large bowl, combine 1 cup flour, ½ cup sugar, the salt and yeast. Blend well.

In a small saucepan, heat milk and butter until very warm (120° to 130°). Add warm liquid, vanilla and eggs to flour mixture. Blend on low speed until moistened. Beat 2 minutes on medium speed. By hand, stir in enough remaining flour to form a soft dough. Cover loosely with greased plastic wrap and a cloth towel. Let rise in warm place until light and doubled in size, 30 to 40 minutes. (Dough will be sticky.)

Grease 2 large baking sheets. In small bowl, combine nuts, remaining ½ cup sugar and the cinnamon; blend well. Drop about ¼ cup dough into nut mixture, thoroughly coating. Stretch dough to about 8 inches in length; twist into desired shape. Place on greased baking sheets. Repeat with remaining dough. Cover and let rise in warm place about 15 minutes.

Uncover dough and bake at 375° for 8 to 16 minutes or until light golden brown. Immediately remove from baking sheets; cool on wire racks. Serve warm. Makes 12 rolls.

1940

Sloppy Joes

1 pound ground beef
½ cup chopped onion
¼ cup chopped green pepper
1 can (15 ounces) tomato sauce
¼ cup chili sauce
2 teaspoons vinegar
1 teaspoon chili powder
Salt and pepper to taste

These sandwiches, some say, originated during the '40s. Perhaps, they were one more way to extend ground beef during the shortages of World War II. Whether the name "Joe" comes from the recipe originator or the generic all-American Joe is unknown, but the "sloppy" probably refers to the loose meat filling. Whatever the source, it remains the quintessential treat for tailgates and teen parties.

Cook ground beef with onion and green pepper until meat is no longer pink. Drain off drippings. Add remaining ingredients, blending well. Cover and simmer, stirring occasionally, until thickened, about 15 minutes. Spoon onto hamburger buns. Makes about 6 servings.

Food prices at the end of the decade included: milk, 21¢ per quart; bread, 15¢ per pound; eggs, 80¢ per dozen; Cokes, 5¢ each. At the same time, take-home pay after taxes ranged from $3,000 a year for steel workers to $10,000 for a dentist.

The posh Le Pavillion opened in New York, offering a three-course luncheon for $1.75.

Stuffed Green Peppers

4 green peppers
½ pound ground beef
½ cup chopped onion
2 cans (8 ounces each) tomato sauce
1 cup water
1 can (11 ounces) whole-kernel
  corn, drained
½ cup instant rice
1 teaspoon Worcestershire sauce
Salt and pepper to taste

Stuffed peppers were a popular way to extend meat during World War II.

   Slice tops from green peppers and remove ribs and seeds. Place peppers in a large pot of boiling water and cook 5 minutes. Drain and cool under cold running water. Drain upside down.

   Chop pepper tops. In a large skillet, sauté ground beef, onion and chopped pepper until meat is no longer pink. Drain off drippings. Stir in tomato sauce, water, corn, rice and seasonings. Bring to a boil, then cover and simmer gently until rice is tender and mixture has thickened, about 20 minutes. Stir occasionally to keep mixture from sticking.

   Place peppers upright in a deep casserole. Spoon ground beef mixture into peppers, placing any extra mixture around and over the peppers. Bake at 350°, uncovered, 25 to 30 minutes or until browned. Makes 4 servings.

The jingle "I'm Chiquita Banana, and I've come to say, bananas have to ripen in a certain way..." was heard over the airwaves for the first time.

⚬⚬⚬

The cake mix was born in 1949.

1940

Named after Count
Paul Stroganoff of
Russia, this dish dates
to the late 1800s or
maybe even earlier.
It was after the war,
however, that the dish
became popular, and
every self-respecting
gourmet had a recipe
in his/her file box to
serve and impress
dinner guests.

Beef Stroganoff

1½ pounds top sirloin steak, cut into cubes
¼ cup flour
½ teaspoon salt
⅛ teaspoon pepper
4 tablespoons butter or margarine, divided
½ cup chopped onion
½ pound fresh mushrooms, sliced
1½ cups beef broth
¾ cup sour cream, at room temperature
Cooked noodles

Dredge steak cubes in flour that has been
seasoned with salt and pepper. In a large
frying pan, heat 2 tablespoons butter until
hot. Add beef cubes and brown well on all
sides. Remove beef. Add remaining butter to
frying pan. Add onion and mushrooms; cook,
stirring, until softened.

Add beef broth to pan. Return meat to
pan with any accumulated juices. Cover and
simmer gently until meat is fork-tender, about
30 minutes.

Slowly stir in sour cream. Heat through,
but do not boil. Serve over hot cooked
noodles. Makes about 6 servings.

1940-1949 FACTS 1940-1949

*Le Petit Cordon Bleu cooking
school opened in New York,
charging $21 for six lessons.
The school that would become
The Culinary Institute of America
opened as a small storefront
school in New Haven, CT
with 50 students.*

Orange Chiffon Cake

2¼ cups sifted cake flour
1½ cups sugar
1 tablespoon baking powder
1 teaspoon salt
½ cup vegetable oil
5 egg yolks
½ cup cold water
¼ cup orange juice
3 tablespoons grated orange peel
8 egg whites (1 cup), at room temperature
½ teaspoon cream of tartar

Sift together the flour, sugar, baking powder and salt; place in a large mixing bowl. Make a well in the center and add oil, egg yolks, water, orange juice and orange peel. Beat with a spoon until smooth.

In a mixing bowl, beat egg whites and cream of tartar until stiff peaks form. Gradually pour the yolk mixture into the whites, folding gently with a spatula until just combined. Pour batter into an ungreased 10-inch tube pan and bake at 325° for 65 to 70 minutes or until the top springs back when lightly touched with a finger.

Immediately invert the pan on pan legs, a funnel or bottle and let the cake stand until completely cooled. Serve plain, with fruit or frosted, as desired.

General Mills introduced the chiffon cake in 1948, calling it "the cake discovery of the century." A Los Angeles insurance salesman named Harry Baker had invented the cake some 20 years earlier. He mixed salad oil into his cake batter instead of butter or vegetable shortening. Baker sold the cake at the Hollywood Brown Derby and other outlets and tried to sell his recipe to General Mills during the war. The flour company declined until Baker baked the cake for company executives after the war. Tasting did the trick!

General Mills introduced the cake on its Betty Crocker radio show and advertised the new invention widely. Sales of its cake flour rose 20 percent after the recipe was published.

The flavors were manifold: lemon, orange, chocolate, spice, banana, peppermint, coffee, mocha, pineapple and coconut, to name some.

1940

Immensely popular in the '40s and '50s in a variety of flavors, pudding cakes were marked by a soft cake that rose through a gooey sauce as they baked.

Chocolate Pudding Cake

1 cup flour
2 teaspoons baking powder
½ teaspoon salt
2 tablespoons cocoa
⅔ cup sugar
½ cup milk
½ cup chopped walnuts
2 tablespoons butter or margarine, melted
1 teaspoon vanilla
½ cup firmly packed brown sugar
¼ cup sugar
3 tablespoons cocoa
1 teaspoon vanilla
¼ teaspoon salt
1 cup boiling water

Sift together the flour, baking powder, ½ teaspoon salt, 2 tablespoons cocoa and ⅔ cup granulated sugar. Combine the milk, nuts, melted butter and 1 teaspoon vanilla. Pour into a well-greased 1-quart casserole.

Combine brown sugar, ¼ cup granulated sugar, 3 tablespoons cocoa, 1 teaspoon vanilla and ¼ teaspoon salt. Spread over the batter. Slowly pour boiling water over all. Do not stir. Bake, uncovered, at 350° for 30 minutes. Cover and bake 30 minutes more.

Best served warm with whipped cream or ice cream. Spoon the cake into serving dishes, then spoon some of the pudding mixture over the top. Makes 4 to 6 servings.

Lindy's Cheesecake

1 cup flour
¼ cup sugar
1 teaspoon grated lemon peel
1 egg yolk
¼ teaspoon vanilla
½ cup (1 stick) butter, chilled
Water, if needed

Cheesecakes are centuries old, but Lindy's restaurant in New York City put it on the culinary map them the 1940s. A smooth, rich cheesecake with a pastry crust, Lindy's recipe became the standard bearer for all New York cheesecakes. It was also in the '40s when Chicago baker Charles Lubin introduced a refrigerated cheesecake and named it after his daughter, Sara Lee.

In the work bowl of a food processor, place the flour, sugar, lemon peel, egg yolk and vanilla. Cut butter into small pieces and add to work bowl. Process until mixture forms a ball. Add water, a teaspoon at a time, if mixture seems dry.

Press mixture into a flat disk, wrap in wax paper and chill 1 hour.

Butter a 9-inch springform pan. Using about ⅓ of the dough, pat onto the bottom of the pan, covering it smoothly and evenly. Bake at 400° about 15 minutes or until golden brown. Cool.

Pat remaining dough evenly around the sides of the pan. Set aside. Raise oven temperature to 550°.

Filling: With a mixer, beat cream cheese and sugar thoroughly. Add flour and citrus peels, mixing well. Add eggs and egg yolks, one at a time, beating well after each addition. Stir in vanilla and cream. Pour into crust and bake 12 to 15 minutes. Reduce temperature to 200° and bake 1 hour. Turn off oven and let cheesecake remain in oven until cooled. Refrigerate overnight before serving. Makes 16 servings.

Filling

5 packages (8 ounces each) cream cheese, softened
1¾ cups sugar
3 tablespoons flour
1½ teaspoons each grated lemon and orange peels
5 eggs
2 egg yolks
½ teaspoon vanilla
¼ cup whipping cream

1940

Strawberries Romanoff

Auguste Escoffier, the famed chef at the Carlton Hotel in London in the late 1800s, may have invented this dessert, but "Prince" Mike Romanoff gets credit for the name. The owner of Romanoff's restaurant in Los Angeles claimed to be a descendent of a royal Russian family. The dish had its heyday in the 1940s. Traditionally it is flavored with orange juice and curacao, though many variations exist.

1 quart fresh strawberries
¼ cup sugar
⅓ cup orange juice
⅓ cup curacao, Cointreau or Grand Marnier
Whipped cream or ice cream

Wash and hull berries. Toss with sugar and let stand 10 minutes. Add orange juice and curacao; toss to combine. Cover and refrigerate several hours. Spoon into individual serving dishes and top with whipped cream or ice cream. Makes 4 to 6 servings.

Maurice and Richard McDonald opened a hamburger stand in California in 1948. Within a few years, with the help of a milkshake machine salesman named Ray Kroc, the brothers had franchised the McDonald name. By the end of the century, there were 24,500 restaurants in 115 countries.

1950 to 1959

In the '50s, Americans loved Lucy, Lipton soup and life in the suburbs. GIs returning home from World War II had gotten married, had children and built modern homes on the outskirts of town.

Kitchens were equipped with shiny ranges, refrigerators with freezers, even dishwashers – some in color for the first time – and wonderful timesaving gadgets.

Women – by this time known as homemakers rather than housewives – did the cooking, but it no longer was drudgery. Convenience foods were sprouting faster than lawns in suburban backyards. And they were readily available in neighborhood supermarkets, which stocked about 4,000 different items.

Money was plentiful to buy big roasts for Sunday dinner or cake mixes and canned goods for busy midweek meals.

The '50s have been called the "casserole decade," thanks in large part to the wide assortment of canned soups on the market. Cooks discovered that the creamed soups could be used not only as soups but also as binders in casseroles or as sauce with meat. Green bean bake, hamburger stroganoff and chicken and rice bake – all made with canned soup – were staples on American tables.

No apologies needed. In fact, cooking with convenience food was considered chic, sometimes even "gourmet."

Epicures of the time were serving Baby Borscht – made with baby food – crab and cheese soufflé featuring Velveeta, tomato aspic with bottled French dressing and cake made with fruit cocktail.

Bottled, canned and packaged foods were an easy way for cooks to delve into "foreign" or exotic cooking.

With money and leisure time available, Americans were traveling more, reading Gourmet magazine and trying recipes from James Beard and Dione Lucas.

Home cooks prepared Baked Alaska, chicken divan and spread out elaborate Scandinavian smorgasbords and Hawaiian luaus.

Husbands, meanwhile, were cooking for the first time – on their backyard grills. He-men were throwing steaks, hamburgers, wieners and ham and pineapple kebabs onto the fire.

Television – remember I Love Lucy, Father Knows Best and Lassie? – dominated home life, and Americans ate dinner and entertained in front of the tube.

Swanson's TV Dinner of turkey, stuffing, gravy, peas and sweet potatoes cost 98¢, was easy to eat on a TV tray and involved no cleanup.

For TV parties, California Dip, made from Lipton dry onion soup mix and sour cream, and Chex Mix were as necessary as rabbit ears.

Chex Mix

¼ cup (½ stick) butter or margarine
1¼ teaspoons seasoned salt
4½ teaspoons Worcestershire sauce
1 cup mixed salted nuts
1 cup thin pretzel sticks
8 cups assorted Chex brand cereals
  (corn, wheat and rice)

Heat oven to 250°. Place butter in a large shallow roasting pan and place in the oven to melt. Mix in seasoned salt and Worcestershire sauce. Add nuts, pretzel sticks and cereals, tossing to coat well with the butter.

Bake uncovered for 1 hour, stirring every 15 minutes. Spread on paper towels to drain; cool to room temperature. Store in an airtight container. Makes about 9 cups.

Ralston Purina dreamed up this recipe in the '50s to extend the use of its Chex brand cereals. Undoubtedly the company never dreamed it would be the hit it became. Even today, hostesses everywhere put out a bowlful at parties.

Green Bean Bake

1 can (10¾ ounces) cream of
  mushroom soup
½ cup milk
1 teaspoon soy sauce
Pinch of black pepper
2 cans (1 pound each or: 15½ ounces each)
  green beans, drained
1 can (2.8 ounces) French fried onions,
  divided

Lightly grease a 1½-quart casserole. Combine soup, milk, soy sauce and pepper in the casserole. Stir in green beans and half the onions. Bake, uncovered, at 350° for 25 minutes or until bubbling. Stir. Top with remaining onions and bake 5 minutes more. Makes 6 servings.

Created by Campbell Soup Co. in 1955, this simple recipe remains a classic. It represents the epitome of '50s cooking, a creamed soup casserole that's easy to make.

An inspiration of the '50s, this salad may have originated in the kitchens of Stokely-Van Camp, although its history is unclear. When men took to the backyard grills during the decade, this salad was a popular side dish along with burgers or steak and foil-wrapped garlic bread.

Three Bean Salad

1 can (15½ ounces) cut green beans, drained
1 can (15½ ounces) wax beans, drained
1 can (15½ ounces) red kidney beans, drained
½ cup chopped celery
½ cup chopped green pepper
½ cup chopped onion
3 tablespoons sugar
⅓ cup olive or vegetable oil
¼ cup vinegar
Salt and pepper to taste

In a large salad bowl, combine beans, celery, green pepper and onion. In a screw-top jar, combine sugar, olive oil, vinegar, salt and pepper. Close lid and shake well to combine; pour over salad, tossing to coat. Cover and chill several hours before serving. Makes 8 to 10 servings.

California Dip

1 envelope dry onion soup mix
2 cups (1 pint) sour cream

Stir soup mix into sour cream. Chill at least 1 hour. Serve with chips, crackers or raw vegetables. Makes 2 cups.

If Chex Mix wasn't simple enough for a hostess, this dip surely was. A combination of dry onion soup mix and sour cream, the recipe was invented by a California cook in 1954, two years after Lipton's dry onion soup mix hit the market. When Lipton heard about it, they began publishing the recipe on their packages of soup mix. Today a pre-mixed dip is available in most dairy departments, but "scratch" cooks continue to mix their own.

Calorie-free ginger ale, sweetened with cyclamates, hit the market and became the first palatable sugar-free soft drink.

Angel Biscuits

1 envelope active dry yeast
2 tablespoons warm water (105° to 115°)
5 cups flour
¼ cup sugar
1 tablespoon baking powder
1 teaspoon baking soda
1½ teaspoons salt
1 cup vegetable shortening
2 cups buttermilk

Dissolve yeast in warm water. Set aside. In a large bowl, combine flour, sugar, baking powder, soda and salt. Cut in shortening with a pastry blender until mixture resembles coarse crumbs. Mix in buttermilk and yeast mixture until dough holds together. Knead lightly 30 seconds. Chill, covered, 1 hour or overnight.

Remove the amount of dough desired and roll to a thickness of ½-inch. Cut with a biscuit cutter and place on a lightly greased baking sheet. Let rise 30 minutes. Bake at 400° for 10 minutes or until golden brown. Makes about 2½ dozen biscuits.

Legend says these light, airy biscuits came about when commercial yeast was newly available but not fully trusted by home cooks. The cooks added baking powder and baking soda to ensure success. Whether or not it's true, historians date the recipe nearer to the '50s, when Southern cooks bragged about their new biscuit recipe made with yeast. The dough will keep in the refrigerator for about a week.

1950 · 1959 FACTS 1950 · 1959

Nutrition guru Adelle Davis propelled the health-food movement with the publication of **Let's Eat Right to Keep Fit.** *Millions of copies were sold despite the book's unsubstantiated claims and factual errors.*

1950

Sweet and Sour Pork

Once Trader Vic's introduced Californians to Hawaiian fare (or the restaurant's interpretation of it), word soon spread to all Americans. What could be more fun than grass skirts, palm leaves, exotic rum drinks in hollowed coconut shells and foods flavored with pineapple and soy sauce? Who cared if it was authentic? Chunks of canned ham on skewers with pineapple, hot dogs in sweet and sour sauce, baked bananas, chicken cooked in coconut milk – most anything with a South Seas flair was foreign and therefore exotic. Sweet and sour pork was a classic of the era.

2 pounds lean pork cubes, cut into cubes
2 tablespoons vegetable oil
½ teaspoon salt
2 tablespoons soy sauce, divided
½ cup water
1 medium onion, peeled and cut into wedges
1 large green pepper, cut into cubes
1 can (20 ounces) pineapple chunks
¼ cup firmly packed brown sugar
2 tablespoons cornstarch
¼ cup cider vinegar
Hot cooked rice

Brown pork on all sides in hot vegetable oil. Drain off any drippings. Add salt, 1 tablespoon soy sauce and water to the pan. Cover and simmer until pork is almost tender, about 45 minutes. Add onion and green pepper to pan and cook 15 minutes.

Drain pineapple, reserving the juice. Combine brown sugar and cornstarch, mixing well. Stir in vinegar, pineapple juice and remaining tablespoon of soy sauce. Add pineapple chunks to pan. Add sauce mixture and cook over medium heat, stirring constantly, until mixture thickens and boils. Serve over rice. Makes 6 to 8 servings.

1954 food prices included: round steak, 92¢ per pound; bread, 17¢ per pound loaf; coffee, $1.10 per pound; eggs, 60¢ per dozen; and butter, 72¢ per pound.

Hamburger Stroganoff

1½ pounds ground beef
½ cup chopped onion
¼ teaspoon paprika
1 jar (4 ounces) sliced mushrooms, drained
1 can (10¾ ounces) cream of mushroom soup
1 cup sour cream
2 teaspoons browning sauce, such as
 Kitchen Bouquet, optional
Hot cooked noodles

For homemakers who had tired of kitchen drudgery, this dish offered a quick and easy step toward "gourmet." It also was more affordable than the classic beef Stroganoff. Hostesses of the '50s loved it.

In a large skillet, sauté ground beef and onion until meat is no longer pink. Drain off drippings. Add paprika, mushrooms and soup, mixing thoroughly. Cook over low heat, stirring occasionally, about 15 minutes. Stir in sour cream and browning sauce if desired, blending thoroughly. Heat through but do not boil. Serve over noodles. Makes 6 to 8 servings.

Demand for yogurt, wheat germ, brewer's yeast and other "wonder foods" skyrocketed following the publication of Look Younger, Live Longer.

1950-1959
• FACTS •
1950-1959

∞∞∞

The Basic Seven Food Groups was simplified to become the Basic Four.

∞∞∞

In 1957, margarine consumption outpaced butter for the first time.

1950

German Sweet Chocolate Cake

This recipe was popular in Texas and Oklahoma before General Foods caught wind of it. The company began publishing the recipe on the label of its Baker's Sweet Chocolate in 1958, and the cake became a nationwide hit. It remains so to this day.

2 cups sifted flour
1 teaspoon baking soda
¼ teaspoon salt
1 package (4 ounces) German's
  Sweet Chocolate
½ cup water
1 cup (2 sticks) butter or margarine,
  softened
2 cups sugar
4 eggs, separated
1 teaspoon vanilla
1 cup buttermilk

Line the bottoms of three 9-inch round cake pans with wax paper and set aside.

Sift flour, soda and salt together; set aside. Break up chocolate and combine with water in a microwave-safe bowl. Microwave on high power until chocolate is almost melted, stirring occasionally. Stir until chocolate is completely melted. (If preferred, combine chocolate with boiling water and stir until chocolate is melted.)

In a mixing bowl, combine butter and sugar; beat until fluffy. Beat in egg yolks, one at a time, until well combined. Blend in vanilla and melted chocolate mixture.

Add flour mixture alternately with buttermilk, beginning and ending with flour and beating after each addition.

In a separate bowl with clean beater, beat egg whites until stiff. Fold into batter.

Pour into prepared pans and bake at 350° for 30 minutes or until the cakes spring back when lightly touched and begin to pull away from sides of pans.

Cool in pans 15 minutes, then turn out onto wire racks to cool completely. Peel off wax paper.

Frosting: In a medium saucepan, combine evaporated milk, sugar, egg yolks, butter and vanilla. Cook over medium heat, stirring, until thickened and caramel-colored, about 12 minutes. Remove from heat and stir in coconut and pecans. Beat until of spreading consistency.

Place one cake layer on cake plate and spread ⅓ of the frosting on top. Top with second cake layer and spread ⅓ of the frosting on top. Top with final layer and spread the remaining frosting on top. Leave the cake sides plain.

Coconut-Pecan Frosting

1½ cups evaporated milk
1½ cups sugar
4 egg yolks, lightly beaten
¾ cup (1½ sticks) butter or margarine, softened
1½ teaspoons vanilla
2 cups flaked coconut
1½ cups chopped pecans

1950-1959 • **FACTS** • *1950-1959*

Sweetening the breakfast table for the first time were Sugar Pops, Frosted Flakes, Sugar Smacks, Cocoa Krispies, Cocoa Puffs and Frosty O's. Trix, introduced by General Mills, was 46.6% sugar.

1950

Apparently this recipe really did come from the First Lady. It's just as popular today as it was in the '50s.

Mamie Eisenhower's Million-Dollar Fudge

4½ cups sugar
Pinch of salt
2 tablespoons butter or margarine
1 can (12 ounces) evaporated milk
1 package (12 ounces) semi-sweet chocolate chips
3 packages (4 ounces each) German's Sweet Chocolate
1 jar (7 ounces) marshmallow crème
2 cups chopped nuts, optional

Combine sugar, salt, butter and evaporated milk in a heavy saucepan. Bring to a boil and boil 6 minutes. Meanwhile, place chocolate chips, sweet chocolate, marshmallow crème and nuts, if desired, in a large bowl. Pour boiling syrup over ingredients in bowl. Beat until chocolate is melted and marshmallow crème is incorporated. Pour into a buttered 13-by-9-inch pan. Let stand until firm. Cut into squares.

1950·1959
FACTS
1950·1959

The electric skillet and a home-sized microwave oven made their debut.

⌘⌘⌘

Chicken Ramen – the first instant Chinese noodle product was introduced.

1960 to 1969

French food captured America's attention in the '60s, thanks to the Kennedys and Julia Child. When John and Jackie arrived at the White House in 1961, they hired a French chef for the first time to head the mansion's kitchens.

If the first family's elegant dinner parties didn't inspire home cooks, then Julia Child's first cookbook and television show did. Her detailed printed instructions for chocolate mousse and coq au vin made these French classics doable for the average cook. And Child's foibles on camera made cooking seem fun. Thanks to her, cooks bought fish poachers, copper bowls and wire whisks. They switched from margarine to butter and took cooking classes to improve their skills.

The 1964 World's Fair in New York opened America's eyes to more foreign cuisines. Visitors tasted Indian, Korean, Japanese and African foods – many for the first time – and they fell in love with the waffles served in the Belgian village.

The Immigration Act that went into effect in 1968 unlocked the gates for a flood of foreigners, who brought their food ways with them.

The restaurants they started whetted America's appetite for shish kebabs, sukiyaki and Szechwan peppercorns.

Pocketbooks were full so cooks plucked international ingredients from supermarket shelves and bought wines and liqueurs for the first time to enhance their so-called "gourmet" dishes.

On the weekends, cooks of the '60s could whip up a decent boeuf bourguignon or shrimp tempura to impress friends, but they continued to use convenience foods during the week.

At the beginning of the decade, nearly a third of married women were working outside of the home, and the number continued to grow. More than ever, time-cramped cooks turned to cake mixes, canned soups and processed cheeses to feed their families.

And if they didn't have time to dust Shake 'n Bake on pork chops, they could choose from a growing field of fast-food establishments.

The decade, of course, was not all cake mixes and champagne. It also was the time of the Vietnam War, hippies, anti-establishment causes and the renewal of the health-food movement.

Rachel Carson's <u>Silent Spring</u> made Americans aware of pollution, and Euell Gibbons' <u>Stalking the Wild Asparagus</u> contributed to a back-to-nature lifestyle.

Young people turned away from Wonder Bread and canned vegetables, choosing whole-grain breads and organic vegetables instead.

Shakes made with raw milk, and burgers made with brown rice and carrots had a following among the health-conscious.

Despite a passing interest in soul food in the '60s, American food was mostly homogenized by the end of the decade. Regional dishes and the recipes of previous generations were abandoned in favor of nouveau gourmet, foreign fare and the indomitable souped-up casserole.

Gazpacho

1 medium onion, cut into quarters
2 cloves garlic, peeled
1 large cucumber, peeled, seeded and
  cut into quarters
1 green pepper, cored and cut into quarters
8 large ripe tomatoes, peeled, seeded
  and cut into quarters
¼ cup olive oil
¼ cup red wine vinegar
1 cup cold water
½ teaspoon salt, or to taste
⅛ teaspoon pepper, or to taste

This cold Spanish soup was hot during the '60s, partly because of America's infatuation with blenders and its fixation on foreign foods.

Garnish

½ cup peeled, seeded and finely chopped
  fresh tomato
½ cup seeded and finely chopped
  green pepper
½ cup peeled, seeded and finely chopped
  cucumber
2 cups prepared croutons

Place onion, garlic, cucumber, green pepper and tomatoes in a blender and blend until puréed. Place in a bowl and add olive oil, vinegar, water and seasonings. Chill several hours or overnight.

At serving time, ladle puréed mixture into soup bowls and garnish with chopped vegetables and croutons. Makes about 6 servings.

1960-1969 FACTS

*Lutèce opened in New York
with Christofle silver
and Baccarat crystal. A prix
fixe lunch cost $8.50.*

1960 | Spinach Salad

1 package (6 ounces) fresh spinach
3 slices bacon, cooked until crisp
2 cups seasoned croutons
2 hard-cooked eggs, peeled and diced

Spinach salads were dressed with a hot bacon dressing during the '50s. Then Americans discovered that the blender could produce a splendid sweet and sour dressing for spinach. This recipe became the rage, even for those who normally wouldn't touch the leafy green stuff.

Combine Dressing ingredients in a blender container. Blend until well combined.

In a salad bowl, tear spinach. Crumble bacon and add to bowl with croutons and eggs. Pour some of the dressing over the spinach, tossing to coat. Refrigerate remaining dressing. Makes 6 to 8 servings.

Dressing
⅔ cup sugar
1 teaspoon salt
Pepper to taste
½ teaspoon celery seeds
2 tablespoons prepared mustard
⅓ cup vinegar
⅓ cup vegetable oil
⅓ cup water
¼ cup chopped onion

Bridgford Foods Corp. introduced the first frozen bread dough after a baker accidentally kept some dough in the freezer overnight and discovered it baked well.

Zucchini Bread

1960

3 cups flour
1 teaspoon baking soda
1 teaspoon baking powder
1 teaspoon salt
1 tablespoon ground cinnamon
3 eggs
2 cups sugar
1 cup vegetable oil
2 cups shredded zucchini, *see note below*
2 teaspoons vanilla
1 cup chopped walnuts

Grease and flour two 9-by-5-inch loaf pans. Combine flour, soda, baking powder, salt and cinnamon. In another bowl, beat eggs, sugar, oil, zucchini and vanilla. Add dry ingredients and nuts, blending thoroughly.

Pour into prepared pans and bake at 325° for 1 hour or until a toothpick inserted into the center comes out clean.

Let loaves cool in pans 15 minutes, then remove and let cool completely on wire racks.

Note: The zucchini does not have to be peeled. If the squash is large, cut in half horizontally and scrape out the seeds.

Home gardeners discovered zucchini in the '60s. Unfortunately, few realized what a prolific crop the summer squash could be. When the zucchini grew to the size of baseball bats before the gardeners could pick them, they became desperate for recipes to use them. Zucchini bread was the most popular choice because the huge, seedy squash could be used, the bread was moist and delicious, and leftover loaves could be frozen. Cooks even discovered they could freeze the shredded zucchini and make the bread another day.

Granny Smith apples, named after an Australian woman, arrived on U.S. shores.

Kellogg's introduced Apple Jacks cereal, which was 55% sugar.

1960-1969 · FACTS · 1960-1969

1960

Dilly Casserole Bread

2 to 2⅔ cups flour, divided
2 tablespoons sugar
2 teaspoons instant minced onion
2 teaspoons dill seed
1 teaspoon salt
¼ teaspoon baking soda
1 envelope active dry yeast
¼ cup water
1 tablespoon butter or margarine
1 cup cream-style cottage cheese
1 egg
2 teaspoons butter or margarine, melted

Mix 1 cup flour with the sugar, onion, dill seed, salt, soda and yeast in a large mixing bowl. Heat water, 1 tablespoon butter and the cottage cheese in a small saucepan until very warm (120° to 130°). Add warm liquid and egg to mixer; beat on low speed until flour is moistened. Raise mixer speed to medium and beat 3 minutes.

By hand, stir in enough remaining flour to form a stiff batter. Cover and let rise in warm place 45 to 60 minutes, until doubled in bulk.

Grease a 1½- to 2-quart casserole. Stir batter down and turn into casserole. Cover and let rise until light and doubled in bulk, 30 to 45 minutes.

Uncover and bake at 350° for 30 to 40 minutes, until golden brown and hollow-sounding when tapped. Immediately remove bread from casserole and set on wire rack. Brush with melted butter.

The "Truth in Packaging" law was passed.

1960-1969 FACTS 1960-1969

Swiss Cheese Fondue

1 clove garlic, cut in half
2 cups dry white wine
½ pound Gruyere cheese, shredded
½ pound Swiss cheese, shredded
2 tablespoons cornstarch
1 loaf French bread, cut into cubes

Rub the cut clove of garlic inside the fondue pot. Discard garlic. Pour wine into the pot and heat over medium heat until it begins to simmer. Meanwhile toss cheeses with cornstarch.

Toss cheese mixture, a handful at a time, into the wine, stirring constantly and adding more cheese only after cheese in pot has melted. The mixture should be the consistency of a medium white sauce.

Place fondue pot on a burner in the middle of a table. Spear bread cubes with fondue forks and swirl in the cheese. Remove the cheese-coated bread to individual dinner plates. Makes 4 to 6 servings.

Fondue was hip during the '60s. Brides of the decade, who usually received at least one fondue pot as a wedding gift, heated everything from cheese and chocolate to oil and flavored broth for dunking. If enough pots could be found, hostesses could serve an entire meal of fondue. This was among the more simple and classic ideas.

Soup Mix Pot Roast

1 boneless chuck roast, 2 inches thick
1 envelope dry onion soup mix
1 can (10¾ ounces) cream of mushroom soup

Place chuck roast on a large sheet of heavy-duty foil. Sprinkle with dry onion soup mix. Spoon undiluted soup over the top. Cover roast with foil, sealing package securely. Place on a baking sheet and bake at 300° for 3 hours. Makes about 4 servings.

While Julia's fans were whipping up Beef Bourguignon, many working homemakers, struggling with limited time and budgets to feed their families and friends, served this dish. It could be thrown into the oven and forgotten. And it tasted good enough for company.

1960

Julia Child prepared this French stew on her first TV show, The French Chef, *in 1963. She and the dish became famous. This is a simplified version of the classic.*

Beef Bourguignon

1½ pounds lean beef sirloin, cut into cubes
¼ cup flour
¾ teaspoon salt
⅛ teaspoon pepper
2 tablespoons butter
2 tablespoons vegetable oil
1 medium onion, chopped
1 large clove garlic, minced
¾ cup Burgundy or other dry red wine
¾ cup beef broth
1 bay leaf
¼ teaspoon thyme
2 cups frozen small white onions
  or cooked, peeled pearl onions
8 ounces sliced fresh mushrooms
2 tablespoons butter
Hot cooked noodles

Dredge beef cubes in flour that has been seasoned with salt and pepper. In a large skillet, heat 2 tablespoons butter and the oil until hot. Add beef, in batches, to skillet and brown well on all sides. As beef browns, remove to a platter.

Place chopped onion and garlic in the skillet and cook, stirring, until softened. Return meat with any drippings to the pan. Add wine, beef broth, bay leaf and thyme; bring to a boil. Cover, reduce heat and simmer gently until beef is almost tender, about 45 minutes. Add frozen onions and cook 15 minutes more.

Meanwhile in another skillet, sauté mushrooms in 2 tablespoons butter until browned. Add to beef mixture and heat until beef and onions are tender. Remove bay leaf. Serve over cooked noodles. Makes about 4 servings.

Coq au Vin

3 slices bacon, cut into pieces
3 tablespoons butter
1 broiler-fryer chicken (3½ to 4 pounds),
  cut into pieces
½ pound white pearl onions, peeled and
  parboiled, or frozen small white onions
½ pound sliced mushrooms
1 clove garlic, minced
⅓ cup cognac or brandy, warmed
1 cup dry red wine
1 bay leaf
3 sprigs parsley
¼ teaspoon thyme
½ teaspoon salt
⅛ teaspoon pepper
1 tablespoon butter, softened
1 tablespoon flour

Americans were just beginning to use wine in cooking, when Julia Child came along. She made it chic. Her coq au vin (which means chicken in wine) was one of her most popular recipes. Cooks everywhere were buying cognac and red wine to duplicate her French dish. She made it look so easy.

In large heavy skillet, cook bacon until fat is rendered. Remove bacon and add 3 tablespoons butter to the skillet. When hot, add chicken pieces and brown well on all sides. Remove chicken to a platter.

Place onions, mushrooms and garlic in skillet and brown well, stirring occasionally. Pour in warm cognac and carefully ignite it with a long match. When flame dies out, return the bacon and chicken to the pan. Add wine and seasonings. Cover and simmer until chicken is tender, about 45 minutes.

Blend 1 tablespoon butter and flour thoroughly in a small dish. Remove bay leaf and parsley from skillet and add butter/flour mixture, a bit at a time, stirring constantly, until liquid has thickened. Makes about 4 servings.

1960

This was another dish that Julia Child made famous. Her recipe in Mastering the Art of French Cooking *was so detailed, she gave cooks confidence to make it at home. It's impossible to guess how many '60s dinner parties ended with chocolate mousse for dessert. This is a simplified version. It uses raw egg whites, which can cause illness, so buy pasteurized eggs to make it.*

A company dinner might have called for chocolate mousse for dessert, but this quick and easy dessert fit the bill for family dinners and potlucks. Any flavor cake or gelatin can be used.

Chocolate Mousse

8 ounces semi-sweet chocolate
¼ cup strongly brewed coffee or hot water
5 pasteurized eggs, separated
1½ teaspoons vanilla
1 cup whipping cream

In the top of a double boiler over simmering water, melt chocolate in coffee. Lightly beat egg yolks. Add a little of the chocolate mixture to the yolks, beating constantly. Return the mixture to the pan and heat, stirring, until mixture is hot but not bubbling.

Beat egg whites until thick and glossy. Fold egg whites and vanilla into chocolate mixture. Whip cream until stiff and fold it into the mousse. Transfer to a serving dish, cover and chill several hours or overnight. Makes 6 to 8 servings.

Poke Cake

1 box (2-layer size) white cake mix
1 package (4-serving size) lemon flavored gelatin
1 cup boiling water
1 cup cold water
Frozen whipped topping, thawed

Prepare and bake cake mix as directed on package, baking in a greased and floured 13-by-9-inch pan. Cool 10 minutes. Meanwhile, dissolve gelatin in boiling water. Add cold water.

Poke holes in cake at ½-inch intervals with a large fork. Pour warm gelatin slowly over the cake. Refrigerate several hours. Top with whipped topping and serve from the pan. Makes about 12 servings.

1970 to 1979

Real men did eat quiche in the '70s. Real men and nearly everybody else in the country.

Americans, never content to settle for classic preparations, began doctoring the cream-and-egg pie with everything from anchovies to leftovers. It was not until the end of the decade that the dish began to tire.

The "me" generation, as the maturing baby boomers came to be called, indulged themselves on gooey desserts made with Cool Whip, cream cheese or ice cream and on rich entrees such as fettuccine Alfredo and moussaka.

The Bundt pan was ubiquitous, giving shape to Harvey Wallbanger cake, rum cake and Jell-O pudding cake, among a slew of other desserts and breads.

The slow cooker was another hot kitchen item in the '70s. Busy homemakers could throw a chicken and a can of cream-of-something soup into the cooker on the way out the door and have dinner on the table for their families within minutes after they arrived home from work.

Americans' interest in French cooking waned; in its place the cuisine-savvy (now called foodies), adopted Szechwan, Hunan, Italian and Mediterranean as haute. Cioppino, pasta primavera, baklava and moo shu pork were on the lips of trend followers.

If Americans were self-indulgent during the '70s, perhaps it brought relief from the troubling times. Antiwar protests, Watergate *and inflation all called for some kind of comfort.*

The intemperance of the decade had a counter movement, however. The term nouvelle cuisine was coined during the '70s and, although it had its roots in France, came to stand for light, fresh and simple in America.

Alice Waters, who opened her California restaurant Chez Panisse early in the decade, generally is credited with introducing Americans to simple foods made with fresh seasonal ingredients. A newcomer to the restaurant business, she sought out local farmers for the freshest items available.

She and a few other forward-thinking chefs introduced the country to unheard-of salad greens such as Belgian endive, frisee and arugula as well as to fresh herbs, goat cheese and flavorful olive oils.

The salad bar – although rarely as fresh, light or innovative as Waters' offerings – thrived. R. J. Grunts, a restaurant in Chicago, opened one of the first salad bars in 1971 with 40 health-food items. Bars that followed lost the health focus, however, and were stocked with fatty but popular items, such as shredded cheese, bacon bits, fried croutons and thick mayonnaise-based dressings.

Health foods did break into the consciousness of mainstream America, though. Several vegetarian cookbooks appeared, and a vegetarian restaurant in California called Greens opened in 1979 to acclaim.

Whole-grain breads, yogurt, brown rice and bean sprouts were accepted, even by some gourmets. Probably the most widely embraced "health food" was granola. Most granolas of the era were heavy in fat and sugar, but at least America's attention was turning toward health.

Buffalo Chicken Wings

2 dozen chicken wings
Vegetable oil for deep frying
¼ cup (½ stick) butter or margarine
⅓ to ⅔ cup Louisiana hot sauce, to taste
Celery sticks
Blue cheese salad dressing

Americans developed a taste for heat in the '70s. Whether hot wings were the cause or the result is unclear. But the popularity of this appetizer is undisputed. Invented in a bar in Buffalo, NY, fried chicken wings took flight all across the country.

Cut off and discard wing tips. Cut wings at joint. Heat oil in a deep fryer to 375°. Fry wings, a few at a time, until crisp and golden, about 10 minutes. Drain on paper towels.

Melt butter and add hot sauce to taste. Place wings in a large container. Pour the sauce over them and toss thoroughly. Serve warm with celery sticks and blue cheese dressing. Makes 4 to 6 servings.

1970-1979
• FACTS •
1970-1979

Restaurants making a splash during the decade included K-Paul's Louisiana Kitchen in New Orleans, Jean-Louis in Washington, DC, Le Francais near Chicago and Michael's in Los Angeles.

1970

*Restaurants introduced
Americans to this
appetizer. It was
standard menu fare
during the '70s.*

Potato Skins

4 baking potatoes
Vegetable oil for deep frying
Salt
4 to 6 slices bacon, cooked until crisp and
  crumbled
1 cup (4 ounces) shredded Cheddar cheese
¼ cup chopped green onions
Sour cream

Bake potatoes until tender. Cut in half and
scoop out as much pulp as possible, being
careful not to tear the skins. (Save pulp for
another use.)

Heat fat in a deep fryer to 375°. Fry potato
skins until crisp and brown. Drain on paper
towels. Place skins, hollow side up, on a
baking sheet and sprinkle with salt, crumbled
bacon, cheese and onion. Place under a hot
broiler and cook until cheese has melted.
Serve with sour cream. Makes 8 servings.

*The Zagat New York City
Restaurant Survey premiered
with ratings based on customer
satisfaction. Zagat, since, has
grown to cover more than 30
American and foreign cities.*

*Universal Product Codes first
appeared on grocery products,
but acceptance came reluctantly.
Supermarkets balked at the price of
installing scanners, and consumers
complained when prices were
removed from individual items.*

Quiche Lorraine

8 slices bacon
1 unbaked 9-inch pie shell
2 cups shredded Swiss or Gruyere cheese
4 eggs, slightly beaten
1½ cups light cream or half & half
½ teaspoon salt
⅛ teaspoon white pepper
1 tablespoon butter or margarine
Dash of ground nutmeg

Cook bacon until crisp. Drain on paper towels, then crumble and sprinkle over the bottom of prepared pie shell. Sprinkle cheese on top. Beat together the eggs, cream, salt and pepper. Carefully pour over the cheese. Dot with butter and sprinkle with nutmeg. Bake at 375° for 35 to 40 minutes or until a knife inserted near the center comes out clean. Let stand 10 minutes before cutting. Makes 6 to 8 servings.

Everybody was eating quiche in the '70s, for breakfast, brunch, lunch and sometimes even dinner. This version, based on the pies served in the Alsatian region of France, is among the more simple.

Food & Wine *magazine rolled off the presses.*

❧

Le Cirque opened in New York with such specialties as Billy-bi, pasta primavera, piperade and duck terrine with pâté de foie gras. Also new to the world of fine cuisine was Windows on the World, on top of the south tower of the former World Trade Center.

Granola

4 cups old-fashioned rolled oats
¼ cup wheat germ
¼ cup sesame seeds
½ cup shelled sunflower seeds
½ cup slivered almonds
¼ cup flaked coconut
½ cup honey
⅓ cup vegetable oil

Granola had an aura of health about it. With rolled oats, seeds and nuts, it seemed nutritious. It could have been, without the oil and honey that everyone loved.

Line a baking sheet with foil. Combine rolled oats, wheat germ, sesame seeds, sunflower seeds, almonds and coconut. Combine honey and oil; toss with oat mixture, coating thoroughly. Spread mixture evenly on foil-lined pan and bake at 300° for 25 to 35 minutes, stirring once or twice, until golden brown. Cool to room temperature. Store in an airtight container. Makes about 7 cups.

1970-1979 FACTS 1970-1979

Linus C. Pauling created a stir with his book, Vitamin C and the Common Cold, *in which he recommended taking mega doses of ascorbic acid. Frances Lappe also stirred up emotions with* Diet for a Small Planet. *She advocated eating vegetables and beans instead of ecologically wasteful meat. Nathan Pritikin kicked off a crusade for heart-healthy living in* The Pritikin Program for Diet and Exercise.

Layered Salad

1 head iceberg lettuce, chopped
6 hard-cooked eggs, sliced
1 package (10 ounces) frozen peas,
  thawed and patted dry
1 pound bacon, cooked until crisp and crumbled
2 cups (8 ounces) shredded Swiss cheese
1 cup mayonnaise
1 cup sour cream
1 tablespoon sugar
¼ cup finely chopped green onions
Paprika

Hostesses discovered layered salads in the '70s and fell in love with them. The salads were made in advance and refrigerated, could feed a crowd and were pretty and easy to serve on a buffet. That they tasted good was an added plus.

In a large glass bowl, layer lettuce, eggs, peas, bacon and cheese. Combine mayonnaise and sour cream, spread evenly over the top, sealing to the edge of the bowl. Sprinkle with sugar. Garnish top with green onions and paprika. Cover and refrigerate overnight. Serve with a salad fork and spoon to scoop into each layer. Makes about 12 servings.

Hamburger Helper came to rescue harried homemakers. Stove Top stuffing was another timesaver to hit the market.

New York Times *Food Editor, Craig Claiborne and his friend Pierre Franey ate a 31-course dinner at Chez Denis in Paris at a cost of $4,000 with tips. Claiborne's mediocre review in the* Times *brought howls of protest from readers, who criticized such an expenditure when others were hungry.*

1970

Tabbouleh

1 cup uncooked bulgur (cracked wheat)
2 cups boiling water
1 cup finely chopped parsley
2 tablespoons finely chopped fresh mint
1 small onion, finely chopped
2 large ripe tomatoes, chopped
1 small cucumber, diced
¼ cup olive oil
¼ cup lemon juice
½ teaspoon salt

Perhaps it was the health movement of the '60s or the interest in international cuisines in the '70s that brought this Middle Eastern salad to the American table. Whatever the cause, it became quite chic.

Place bulgur in a large bowl and pour boiling water over it. Cover and let stand 1 hour. Fluff with a fork. Stir in parsley, mint, onion, tomatoes and cucumber. In a screw-top jar, combine olive oil, lemon juice and salt. Shake well to blend, then pour over the salad, mixing well. Cover and chill at least 2 hours. Makes 4 to 6 servings.

The Center for Science in the Public Interest was founded in Washington, DC by Michael F. Jacobson. In the next 30 years, his organization became a thorn in the side of food companies as it worked to improve food safety and nutrition.

Slow Cooker Bavarian Stew

1 small onion, chopped
1 clove garlic, minced
4 carrots, peeled and sliced
2 potatoes, peeled and cubed
1 pound beef stew meat
2 tablespoons quick-cooking tapioca
1 can (12 ounces) beer
1 beef bouillon cube
1 teaspoon salt
½ teaspoon pepper

Place ingredients in slow cooker in the order given. Cover and cook on low heat 8 to 10 hours. Makes 4 servings.

Working women loved the slow cooker for its timesaving convenience. All kinds of recipes were developed for the cookers, but their real claim to fame was with main dishes.

Cookbooks from the decade included Classic French Cooking *by Craig Claiborne,* Mastering the Art of French Cooking Volume II *by Julia Child and Simone Beck,* The California Cookbook *by Jeanne Voltz,* How to Eat (and Drink) Your Way Through a French (or Italian) Menu *by James Beard,* The Best of Italian Cookery *by Waverley Root and* Mediterranean Cooking *by Paula Wolfert.*

1970

Szechwan Pork Stir-Fry

Americans were just learning the technique of stir-frying in the '70s. They also were developing a taste for chili peppers. This simplified recipe combines both.

½ pound boneless lean pork
2 teaspoons cornstarch
2 teaspoons soy sauce
2 teaspoons dry sherry
¼ cup peanut oil
8 small dried chili peppers
1 teaspoon minced fresh gingerroot
1 clove garlic, minced
1 small onion, peeled and cut into wedges
1 sweet red pepper, cut into thin strips
1 can (8 ounces) bamboo shoots, drained
Cooked rice

Sauce
1 teaspoon cornstarch
1 teaspoon sugar
2 tablespoons dry sherry
2 tablespoons soy sauce
2 tablespoons water
1 teaspoon rice wine vinegar

1970-1979 · FACTS · 1970-1979

Kikkoman International launched a plant in Wisconsin to brew soy sauce for the American market.

Average U.S. food prices in 1974 included: sugar, 32¢ per pound; bread, 35¢ per pound loaf; and coffee, $1.28 per pound.

Cut pork into thin strips. Combine the 2 teaspoons each of cornstarch, soy sauce and sherry. Add pork, tossing to combine. Let stand 30 minutes.

Combine Sauce ingredients and set aside. Heat oil in a frying pan or wok until hot. Add chili peppers and stir-fry until blackened. Remove peppers from oil and discard.

Place ginger, garlic, onion and red pepper in pan and stir-fry until crisp-tender. Move vegetables to outer rim of pan and add pork to center. Stir-fry until pork is no longer pink. Re-stir Sauce and add to pan with the bamboo shoots. Cook, stirring, until mixture boils and thickens. Serve over rice. Makes about 3 servings.

Two young couples from Boulder, CO picked herbs in the Rockies to flavor their new variety of teas. With product names such as Red Zinger, Morning Thunder and Sleepy Time, Celestial Seasonings was born.

⸎

Chez Panisse opened in Berkeley, CA, with a three-course dinner – pâté maison, duck with olives, and almond tart – for $3.95. The owner, Alice Waters, was a 27-year-old Montessori schoolteacher who borrowed $10,000 from her parents to open the restaurant.

1970

Lemon Bars

Lemon bars were a sensation of the '70s that lasted well into the '90s. It's not surprising why. They were easy to make and combined two favorite tastes – buttery shortbread and tangy lemon. They were so popular that Betty Crocker even produced a lemon bar mix.

1 cup flour
¼ cup confectioners' sugar
½ cup (1 stick) butter, softened
2 eggs
¼ teaspoon baking powder
1 cup sugar
3 tablespoons fresh lemon juice
½ teaspoon grated lemon peel
Pinch of salt
Confectioners' sugar for topping

Combine flour and ¼ cup confectioners' sugar. Cut in butter until mixture resembles cornmeal. Press firmly into the bottom of an ungreased 8-inch square baking pan. Bake at 350° for 20 minutes.

Beat eggs, baking powder, granulated sugar, lemon juice, peel and salt. Pour over baked crust and return to oven for 20 to 25 minutes or until set and lightly browned. Cool and sprinkle with confectioners' sugar. Makes about 9 servings.

Debbi Fields, 21, convinced a banker to provide a loan to start Mrs. Fields Cookies. A year later, Wally Amos, a 39-year-old talent agent, borrowed money from celebrity friends to start Famous Amos Chocolate Chip Cookies.

Rum Cake

1 package (2-layer size) yellow cake mix
1 package (4-serving size) instant vanilla
  pudding mix
4 eggs
½ cup vegetable oil
½ cup water
½ cup dark rum

Glaze
½ cup (1 stick) butter or margarine
¼ cup water
1 cup sugar
½ cup dark rum

Grease and flour a 10-inch Bundt pan or tube pan. Combine cake and pudding mixes in a mixer bowl. Add eggs, oil, water and rum. Beat for 5 minutes, scraping down sides of bowl frequently. Turn into prepared pan and bake at 350° for 50 to 60 minutes or until a pick inserted into the center comes out clean.

Meanwhile, make Glaze: Melt butter in a small saucepan. Add water, sugar and rum. Bring to a boil and boil 5 minutes.

When cake is removed from oven, pour half of the glaze over the top while it is still in the pan. Let the cake stand 20 to 30 minutes, then remove from the pan. Pour remaining glaze over the top. Cool completely.

The Bundt cake pan was first made in the '50s, but it was not widely used until the '60s when a Bundt cake was a finalist in the Pillsbury Bake-Off. Bundt pans flew off the shelves, and scores of new cake recipes were devised to fill them. Many were a variation of the so-called pudding cake, teaming cake and pudding mixes with oil, eggs and some variety of flavorings. Rum cake was one of the popular ones.

Ben & Jerry's cranked up some hip ice cream in Vermont.

Carrot Cake

2 cups flour
2 teaspoons baking powder
1½ teaspoons baking soda
1 teaspoon salt
2 teaspoons ground cinnamon
2 cups sugar
1 cup vegetable oil
4 eggs
2 cups finely grated carrots
1 can (8 ounces) crushed pineapple, drained
1 cup chopped walnuts

Cream Cheese Frosting
½ cup (1 stick) butter or margarine, softened
1 package (8 ounces) cream cheese, softened
1 teaspoon vanilla
1 pound (about 3½ cups) confectioners'
 sugar

Carrot cake dates to early in the 20th century, but the oil-rich, cream cheese-topped cake as it is known today became wildly popular in the '70s. It still maintains a top-notch status.

Grease and flour 3 9-inch round cake pans. Combine flour, baking powder, soda and cinnamon. Set aside.

In a mixing bowl, beat sugar, oil and eggs thoroughly. Add dry ingredients blending just until combined. Fold in carrots, pineapple and walnuts. Divide among prepared pans and bake at 350° for 35 to 40 minutes or until a toothpick inserted into the center comes out clean.

Cool cakes in pans 10 minutes, then remove to wire racks to cool completely.

Cream Cheese Frosting: Cream butter, cream cheese and vanilla until fluffy. Add confectioners' sugar, in batches, and beat until blended.

Spread frosting between layers and on top and sides of cake.

1980 to 1989

In the food scene of the '80s, food wasn't the point. Image was. Maturing baby boomers became yuppies who sought out the most fashionable food and the trendiest restaurants. In what came to be called the Decade of Greed, two-income couples overdosed on luxury cars, high-end condos, frozen "gourmet" meals, the latest appliances and exotic ingredients.

Yuppies didn't have time to cook, at least during the week, but when they did cook, they showed off for guests with hip ingredients such as sun-dried tomatoes, goat cheese, green peppercorns, duck breast, balsamic vinegar and white chocolate. They roasted garlic and red peppers, caramelized onions and seared tuna.

Tony restaurants of the '80s were places to see and be seen – more theater than eatery.

The chefs became celebrities, but the dishes they designed often looked better than they tasted. Colorful and artsy – sometimes shocking – plate presentation ruled. If the plate contained jolting flavor combinations – such as duck liver with orange salad, curly endive and pecans or melon-seed pasta with saffron-infused mussels – theatergoers failed to notice.

Many of the star chefs turned out cookbooks. They were flashy enough to display on a coffee table, but few home cooks could begin to duplicate the recipes, which took days to prepare and called for such oddities as quail demi-glace, blue cornmeal and blood oranges.

Interest in regional cooking caught fire during the decade, fueled by Paul Prudhomme, whose Cajun restaurant, cookbook and spices were hot on the lips of every trend follower. His blackened redfish recipe became so popular that redfish was put on the endangered seafood list.

Americans also discovered Southwestern cooking during the '80s. Mark Miller in New Mexico and Dean Fearing and Stephan Pyles in Texas introduced us to smoked chilies, roasted corn, fruit salsa and cilantro.

Chefs from the Pacific Northwest, the Heartland and New England adopted the idea of using fresh, locally grown foods. Some of them wrote cookbooks, too, or took to the airwaves to promote their region's cooking. While food lovers learned about Dungeness crabs, persimmon pudding and fiddlehead ferns, the dishes of these regions never gained prominence.

By the end of the '80s, Americans were fed up with excess. The stock-market plunge in 1987 and scandals surrounding junk bonds and the savings-and-loan industry hastened the end of avant-garde restaurants and the beginning of comfort food. Foodies who had been playing with penne and polenta now turned to macaroni and cheese and meatloaf.

Microwave ovens were the hot appliance of the decade. Reduced prices made them affordable, and home cooks were eager to duplicate the miraculous demonstrations they saw in appliance stores. It didn't take cooks long to discover, though, that the microwave works better at popping corn and melting butter than it does at cooking pot roast.

The food-health connection, a concept that started to flicker in the '70s, began to flame in the '80s.

The latest research findings made headlines seemingly every day. The aging population took these reports to heart and tried to balance a love of rich food with a goal of health and long life. It wasn't easy because each report seemed to contradict the preceding one.

Fish oils, oat bran, red wine, olive oil, broccoli and wheat germ all had their day of acclaim, but none proved to be the magic bullet Americans hoped for.

Layered Taco Dip

2 ripe avocados
1 tablespoon lemon juice
¾ cup sour cream
¾ cup mayonnaise
1 package (1¼ ounces) taco seasoning mix
1 can (16 ounces) refried beans
2 cups (8 ounces) shredded Cheddar cheese
2 bunches green onions, chopped
2 ripe tomatoes, seeded and chopped
1 can (3½ ounces) pitted black olives,
  drained and chopped

Americans discovered Tex-Mex in the '70s and '80s, and every in-the-know hostess served some variation of this dip. Served with tortilla chips, it was a sure winner at parties.

Peel, pit and mash the avocados. Mix with lemon juice. In another bowl, combine sour cream, mayonnaise and taco seasoning mix. Spread refried beans on a shallow platter or serving dish. Top with avocado mixture, then the sour cream mixture. Sprinkle cheese, onions, tomatoes and olives over the top in that order. Serve cold or at room temperature with tortilla chips.

• 1980-1989 •
FACTS
• 1980-1989 •

Cookbooks of the decade included The Silver Palate Cookbook *by Sheila Lukins and Julee Rosso,* The Chez Panisse Menu Cookbook *by Alice Waters,* The Book of Bread *by Judith and Evan Jones,* Chef Paul Prudhomme's Louisiana Kitchen *and* Foods of Italy *by Giuliano Bugialli,* Marcella's Italian Kitchen *by Marcella Hazan and* Linda McCartney's Home Cooking.

1980

Talk about trendy! This salad includes three chic ingredients of the '80s: mesclun (a gourmet salad mix), goat cheese and well-aged balsamic vinegar.

Mesclun Salad

Balsamic Vinaigrette

2 tablespoons balsamic vinegar
6 tablespoons olive oil
1 clove garlic, minced
½ teaspoon Dijon mustard
Salt and pepper to taste

Place all ingredients in a screw-top jar. Cover and shake well.

Salad

Mixed fresh baby greens and lettuces to make 6 servings
½ cup walnut halves, toasted

Tear greens into a salad bowl. Place walnuts in a dry skillet over medium heat, tossing frequently, until fragrant and lightly toasted. Add to bowl with greens.

Goat Cheese Croutons

French baguette, sliced ¼-inch thick
Olive oil
6 ounces Montrachet or other chèvre cheese, sliced crosswise into 6 rounds

Brush 6 bread slices lightly with olive oil and toast on one side under the broiler. Place a round of cheese on untoasted side of bread slices. Brush cheese with olive oil and broil until cheese starts to brown.

To assemble

Re-mix vinaigrette. Toss with salad mixture and divide equally among 6 salad plates. Top each with a warm cheese crouton. Makes 6 servings.

Black Bean Soup

2 tablespoons olive oil
1 large onion, chopped
2 cloves garlic, minced
1½ tablespoons ground cumin
⅛ teaspoon cayenne pepper
1 teaspoon ground coriander
2 cans (15 to 16 ounces each) black beans
2 cups beef broth
¼ cup dry white wine

It took supermarkets months to catch up with the popularity of Cuban black bean soup. Foodies had to search ethnic markets or health food stores to find either dry or canned black beans. Black beans are still popular today, but they're readily available everywhere.

Heat oil in a soup pot until hot. Add onion and garlic and cook until softened. Stir in cumin, cayenne and coriander; cook, stirring, until fragrant. Add beans, with liquid and the beef broth. Simmer 20 minutes. Stir in wine. (If a thicker soup is desired, remove some of the beans with a slotted spoon. Mash them with the back of a spoon, then return them to the soup pot.) Heat and stir until thickened. Makes 3 to 4 servings.

Oat Bran Muffins

1¾ cups oat bran
¼ cup flour
½ teaspoon salt
½ teaspoon baking soda
¼ teaspoon baking powder
1 teaspoon ground cinnamon
2 egg whites
1 cup skim milk
¼ cup applesauce

When oat bran was found to reduce cholesterol, packages of the cereal flew off supermarket shelves. Muffins were an easy, palatable way to incorporate the grain into the diet.

Combine dry ingredients. In a separate bowl, beat egg whites until frothy. Stir in milk and applesauce. Add liquid ingredients to dry ingredients, mixing just until moist. Fill 12 greased or paper-lined muffin cups. Bake at 400° for 15 minutes or until browned on top. Serve warm. Makes 12 muffins.

Blackened Fish

6 fish fillets, such as cod, pompano,
  red snapper, redfish or bluefish
½ cup (1 stick) butter, melted
3 tablespoons store-bought Cajun
  seasoning mix

   Heat a large cast-iron skillet until hot but
not smoking. Dip fillets in melted butter,
coating both sides. Sprinkle both sides
generously with seasoning mix. Place fillets,
2 or 3 at a time, into the skillet and cook until
well browned on the bottom. Turn over fillets
and cook until browned and cooked through.
Makes 6 servings.

Crab Cakes

½ cup bread crumbs
¼ cup mayonnaise
1 egg, lightly beaten
1 teaspoon Old Bay Seasoning
Dash of Worcestershire sauce
1 pound lump crab meat
Butter for frying

Combine bread crumbs, mayonnaise, egg
and seasonings, blending well. Add crab meat
and toss lightly. Melt butter in a frying pan.
Spoon ¼ cup mounds of crab mixture into
pan, flattening them with a spatula. Brown
well, then carefully turn and brown the other
sides. Serve warm with a spicy mustard or
rémoulade sauce. Makes 5 to 6 servings.

*One problem with Chef
Paul Prudhomme's
famous Blackened
Redfish was that
most home kitchens
couldn't handle the
intense smoke created
when a buttered fillet
was dropped into
a white hot skillet.
Outdoor grills are
sometimes suggested
as an alternative to a
kitchen stove, but it
is difficult to control
the heat and flare-ups
may result. Another
problem is that redfish
is not always available.
This is a reasonable
alternative, and it uses
less butter, too.*

*Crab cakes, long a
staple on Eastern
shores, moved west
into restaurant
kitchens throughout
the country around
the '80s.*

Polenta with Three Cheeses

1 cup yellow cornmeal
1 cup water
3 cups chicken stock, heated to boiling
½ teaspoon salt, or to taste
3 tablespoons butter, divided
⅓ cup Parmesan cheese
⅓ cup shredded fontina cheese
⅓ cup crumbled Gorgonzola cheese

Mix cornmeal and water in a large saucepan. Stir in boiling stock and salt. Bring to a boil, stirring constantly. Reduce heat to a simmer and cook, stirring frequently, until very thick, 10 to 15 minutes. Remove from heat and stir in 2 tablespoons butter and the Parmesan cheese.

Spread ½ of the polenta into a well-greased 9-inch square pan. Dot with half the remaining butter. Sprinkle with fontina cheese. Spread remaining polenta on top. Dot with remaining butter. Sprinkle Gorgonzola cheese on top.

Bake at 350° for 15 to 20 minutes or until hot and bubbly. Cut into squares to serve. Makes about 6 servings.

Previous generations of Americans enjoyed cornmeal mush for breakfast. Hearty, but unglamorous, it fell from favor. Then in the '80s, Americans were introduced to the Italian version of mush, called polenta. It was on the menu at hip restaurants, where chefs served it in a multitude of creative ways. Dressed with goat cheese, Italian sausage or a classic Bolognese sauce, it was glamorous indeed.

Americans spent nearly 20% of their retail food dollar on "light" and "diet" foods.

1980-1989 • 1980-1989 FACTS

By 1985, per capita consumption of artificial sweeteners reached 17 pounds.

White Pizza

½ package (1¼ teaspoons) active dry yeast
⅓ cup warm water
1 to 1¼ cups flour, divided
¼ teaspoon sugar
¼ teaspoon salt
¼ teaspoon garlic powder
¼ teaspoon onion powder
1 tablespoon olive oil

Forget the tomato sauce and pepperoni; pizzas of the '80s featured trendy gorgonzola, smoked salmon, sun-dried tomatoes, barbecued chicken, caramelized onions or most anything that could sit on a crust. Thin crusts, as crisp as crackers, also were popular, especially in Chicago, known previously for its deep-dish pizzas.

Dissolve yeast in warm water. Add ½ cup of the flour, the sugar, seasonings and olive oil; beat with a mixer about 1 minute or until smooth. By hand or with a dough hook, stir in enough additional flour to make a soft dough. Cover and let stand 5 minutes.

With greased hands, spread dough on a greased 14-inch pizza pan. Bake in a preheated 425° oven for 15 to 20 minutes. Meanwhile, prepare Toppings.

Remove crust from oven. Brush with garlic-olive oil mixture. Sprinkle cheeses and basil leaves on top. Return pizza to oven for about 10 minutes or until cheeses are melted and crust is crisp and brown. Makes 1 pizza.

Toppings
1 clove garlic, minced
3 tablespoons olive oil
¾ cup crumbled Gorgonzola cheese
¾ cup shredded mozzarella cheese
3 tablespoons thinly sliced fresh basil leaves

Place garlic in olive oil and heat over low heat 5 minutes. Set aside.

Angel Hair Pasta with Pesto Sauce

1 cup firmly packed fresh basil leaves, washed and patted dry

2 cloves garlic, peeled and coarsely chopped

3 tablespoons pine nuts

⅓ cup plus 2 tablespoons olive oil, divided

⅓ cup Parmesan cheese

1 pound angel hair pasta

Salt and pepper to taste

Place basil, garlic, pine nuts, ⅓ cup olive oil and the Parmesan cheese in a blender or food processor and blend until pasty, scraping sides of container occasionally.

Cook pasta in boiling salted water according to package directions. Drain. Toss with 2 tablespoons olive oil. Add pesto sauce and toss again. Season to taste. Makes 4 to 6 servings.

Fresh herbs began appearing in farmers' markets and some supermarkets in the late '70 and early '80s. Among the most popular was basil, which could easily be turned into pesto, an aromatic and rich sauce used for appetizers, pasta or pizza or as a topper for fresh tomatoes. Gardeners with a plentiful supply of basil could make pesto in quantities and refrigerate or freeze it.

Among the restaurant openings in the decade were The Mansion on Turtle Creek in Dallas, An American Place in New York and Charlie Trotter's and Frontera in Chicago.

1980

Rotini with Italian Sausage

1 pound bulk hot Italian sausage
1 tablespoon olive oil
1 large onion, chopped
3 cloves garlic, minced
1 pound rotini
1½ cups reduced-sodium chicken broth
1 tablespoon finely chopped fresh basil
  or 1 teaspoon dried
1 tablespoon finely chopped fresh oregano
  or 1 teaspoon dried
¼ cup Parmesan cheese

Cook sausage in a large skillet, breaking it up with a spatula, until cooked through. Remove sausage with a slotted spoon and set aside. Add olive oil to skillet. Sauté onion and garlic until tender but not brown. Set aside.

Cook rotini in boiling salted water according to package directions.

While pasta is cooking, add chicken broth to the skillet with the onion and garlic and bring to a boil.

Drain pasta thoroughly and add to skillet along with the herbs and reserved sausage. Toss well to combine. Add Parmesan cheese and toss again. Makes 4 to 6 servings.

1980·1989 FACTS 1980·1989

James Beard, the father of American cooking, died in 1985 at age 81.

White Chocolate Mousse with Fresh Raspberries

1980

2 pasteurized eggs, separated
2 teaspoons sugar
½ cup half & half
2 tablespoons light rum
4 ounces white chocolate, chopped
1 cup heavy cream, whipped
Fresh raspberries

Place egg yolks, sugar, half & half and rum in the top of a double boiler over gently simmering water. Cook, stirring constantly, until mixture coats the back of a wooden spoon.

Place chocolate in a glass container and microwave, stirring every 20 to 30 seconds, until melted and smooth. Stir into egg yolk mixture. Let cool to room temperature. Beat egg whites to soft peaks. Gently fold into the chocolate mixture. In another bowl, beat cream to soft peaks. Gently fold into chocolate mixture. Turn into dessert dishes and chill several hours. Garnish with fresh raspberries. Makes 6 servings.

The flourish of white chocolate recipes began in the late '70s. Soon it showed up in mousses, cakes, brownies, truffles, cheesecakes, ice creams and chocolate chip cookies. This recipe calls for uncooked egg whites, which can pose a health risk, so use pasteurized eggs.

General Mills began the Olive Garden chain. Wal-Mart opened its first Super Center, selling fresh meats, produce and baked goods. And actor Paul Newman founded Newman's Own food company and committed the profits to charity.

1980

This old-fashioned dessert resurfaced during the '80s. Chefs served it, as well as cooks yearning for "comfort" food.

Bread Pudding

1-pound loaf of white bread
½ cup raisins
1 cup sugar
2 cups milk
3 eggs
½ cup (1 stick) butter or margarine, melted
1 teaspoon ground cinnamon
¼ teaspoon ground nutmeg
Vanilla Sauce, recipe follows

Grease a 13-by-9-inch baking pan. Tear bread into pieces and place in pan. Sprinkle raisins over the top. Combine sugar, milk and eggs, beating well. Add melted butter, cinnamon and nutmeg. Pour over bread, pressing down with a spatula so that all pieces are moistened.

Bake, uncovered, at 300° for 40 minutes or until pudding is set. Serve warm with warm or room-temperature Vanilla Sauce. Makes 6 to 8 servings.

Vanilla Sauce

½ cup sugar
1½ tablespoons cornstarch
1 cup water
2 tablespoons butter or margarine
2 teaspoons vanilla

In a small saucepan, combine sugar and cornstarch. Add water, mixing well. Cook over medium heat, stirring, until thickened and bubbly. Boil 1 minute. Remove from heat; stir in butter and vanilla.

1990 to 1999

As the 20th century came to a close, Americans came full circle. As at the end of the 1800s, people were concerned about the relationship between food and health. At times, the concern bordered on paranoia.

It wasn't enough to count calories; Americans counted fat grams. It wasn't enough to eat a balanced diet; Americans had to eat soluble fiber and omega-3 fatty acids.

Each time a new scientific study pointed to a link between food and disease, Americans changed their shopping list. Beef was crossed out; chicken was added. Forget butter and margarine; stock up on olive oil.

Americans ate fish oil, wheat germ, garlic and alfalfa sprouts. Some even began drinking red wine for the first time in the hope it might reduce the risk of heart disease.

New foods were "engineered" to promote health. Kellogg's introduced the Ensemble line of food to help lower cholesterol. Procter & Gamble developed a fat-replacer called olestra and made Fat-Free Pringles.

In the '90s, vegetarianism went mainstream, and tofu was no longer a joke. Americans ate for health, not for pleasure.

Foods safety also was a major fear. Antibiotics in milk, nitrates in bacon and E. coli in hamburgers scared people into changing their buying habits. Sales of organic foods became a $17 billion-a-year industry in the United States.

The food scene in the '90s was not all gloomy. Martha Stewart, fashion model turned homemaking icon, showed cooks how to prepare sumptuous dishes and to present them with pizazz. Fans followed her every word as she expanded her realm into a publicly traded empire.

The '90s saw its share of culinary fads and trends. Fusion cooking became a buzzword. No one knew exactly what it meant, but it gave chefs license to combine ingredients from one part of the world with techniques from another.

One trend that struck a chord in main-line America was comfort food. Every chef worth his spuds was turning out mashed potatoes doctored with garlic, wild mushrooms or goat cheese. Meatloaf and chicken potpie – always staples in home kitchens – became fashionable restaurant fare.

Wraps and smoothies were fast-food choices. Adventuresome home cooks, meanwhile, were learning to make tiramisu, grilled portobellos and crème brulee.

During the decade, an increasing number of Americans decided not to cook. With fast foods, frozen foods and takeout foods readily available, they no longer had to.

But their palates became more sophisticated. Food lovers tuned in to the Food Network to watch Emeril Lagasse hurl seasonings onto Spicy Duck Empanadas or to see the Two Hot Tamales whip up Peruvian Stewed Chicken. Foodies also bought cookbooks, not to cook from, but to taste vicariously.

Well-versed in foreign cuisines and exotic ingredients, Americans could differentiate between arugula and frisee, between oyster and chanterelle mushrooms, between star anise and anise seeds.

Farm markets blossomed, not just near farms but also in downtown alleys and suburban parking lots. After years of relying on canned and frozen foods for sustenance, Americans rediscovered the tastes of fresh.

Home computers became a kitchen aid. Recipe swap sites and online food magazines were as near as the execute key. Cooks could buy groceries, specialty food and kitchen equipment without ever leaving the house. And if a novice cook didn't know the difference between baking powder and baking soda, someone on the Web was sure to have the answer.

Who needed Mom to answer cooking questions? If she was a contemporary mom, she probably didn't know how to cook anyway.

Tortilla Soup

4 corn tortillas
Vegetable oil
1 cup chopped onion
2 cloves garlic, minced
1 teaspoon cumin
1 teaspoon chili powder
½ teaspoon oregano
1 can (4 ounces) chopped mild green
  chilies, undrained
6 cups chicken broth
1 can (14½ ounces) diced tomatoes,
  undrained
1½ cups diced cooked chicken
Salt and pepper to taste
4 ounces shredded Monterey Jack cheese
1 tablespoon chopped fresh cilantro

Americans adopted Mexican fare, or at least Tex-Mex fare, in the '90s. One of the favorites was this soup.

Stack tortillas and cut into ¼-inch wide strips. Heat 1 inch of oil in a large frying pan until hot and fry tortilla strips, a few at a time, until crisp. Drain on paper towels and set aside.

Place 1 tablespoon of the vegetable oil in a heavy saucepan or soup pot. Add onion and garlic to pan and sauté until tender. Stir in cumin, chili powder and oregano. Cook, stirring, 30 seconds. Add chilies, chicken broth and diced tomatoes to pan. Cover and simmer 30 minutes. Add chicken and cook 5 minutes more. Taste and add salt and pepper if needed.

Place a handful each of cheese and tortilla strips in soup bowls. Ladle soup on top. Garnish with cilantro. Makes about 6 servings.

1990

This simple salad was a hit during the '90s, but it is still popular today. The secret to its success is top-notch ingredients: garden-ripe tomatoes, fresh mozzarella cheese (available at cheese shops), fresh basil and extra-virgin olive oil.

Tomato, Mozzarella Salad

4 medium-size ripe tomatoes, sliced
8 ounces fresh mozzarella cheese, sliced
2 tablespoons basil leaves, cut into
 julienne strips
Extra-virgin olive oil
Splash of balsamic vinegar, optional
Salt and pepper to taste

On a serving platter, alternate slices of tomatoes and cheese. Sprinkle basil on top. Drizzle olive oil lightly over all. If a more tart taste is desired, sprinkle on a little vinegar. Season to taste. Serve at room temperature. Makes about 6 servings.

Electric bread machines began to rise.

An outbreak of E. coli food poisoning stemming from undercooked hamburgers at a fast-food restaurant brought questions about federal meat inspection practices. New labeling on ground beef ensued, and Americans were urged to eat well-done burgers.

Turkey and Spinach Wraps

¼ cup honey mustard
6 flour tortillas
½ package (6-ounce size) baby spinach,
  as needed
¾ pound thinly sliced turkey
½ cup chopped tomato
½ cup alfalfa sprouts

Spread honey mustard on one side of each tortilla. Cover generously with spinach leaves, then with slices of turkey. Sprinkle tomato and sprouts on top. Roll up tightly, cover and refrigerate. At serving time, cut each wrap diagonally in half. Makes 6 main-dish servings.

Wraps were the "in" sandwiches of the '90s. Wrapped in lavash, a Middle Eastern flatbread, tortillas or pita bread, the sandwich roll-ups were easy to make and easy to eat. And most anything that could be rolled could be used as the filling: roast duck, deli meat, Caesar salad, roasted peppers, cheese and vegetables, to name a few.

The U.S. Department of Agriculture built the Food Pyramid to replace the long-standing Basic Four. At the bottom of the pyramid, representing the largest part of the ideal diet, were breads, cereals and pasta. At the top, representing food to be eaten "sparingly," were fats and sugars.

Focaccia

2½ to 3 cups flour, divided
1 teaspoon sugar
¾ teaspoon salt
1 package quick-rising yeast
2 tablespoons olive oil
1 cup hot water (120° to 130°)
Olive oil for brushing
1½ tablespoons chopped fresh rosemary
  or basil or 1½ teaspoons dried

Mix 1 cup of the flour, the sugar, salt and yeast in a mixing bowl. Add 2 tablespoons olive oil and hot water; beat on low speed until moistened. Beat on medium speed 2 minutes. By hand or with a dough hook, add enough flour to make a soft dough.

Turn dough out onto a floured surface and knead 5 to 10 minutes, until smooth and elastic. Cover with a bowl and let dough rest 5 minutes.

Grease 2 baking sheets. Divide dough in half and shape each into a flat 10- to 12-inch disc. Cover with greased plastic wrap and a towel. Let rise in a warm place until doubled in bulk, 30 to 40 minutes.

Heat oven to 400° and uncover dough. Press indentations in the dough at 1-inch intervals, using fingertips or the handle of a wooden spoon. Brush surface of dough generously with oil. Sprinkle with chopped rosemary. Bake for 15 to 20 minutes or until golden brown. Serve warm or cool.

At the beginning of the decade, Americans were spending an average of $46 per week per household at the grocery store.

Garlic Mashed Potatoes

6 medium-sized potatoes
5 cloves garlic, peeled
Salt
¾ to 1 cup whole milk or half & half, heated
5 tablespoons butter
Pepper

Grandma's favorite side dish came back in vogue in the '90s. Modern versions had more zest. Rich and creamy and flavored with sit-up-and-take-notice garlic, horseradish or wasabi, these spuds didn't need gravy.

Peel potatoes and cut into quarters. Place in a large saucepan with garlic and enough salted water to cover. Cook, covered, until potatoes are fork tender. Drain well.

By hand or with a mixer, mash potato mixture until no longer lumpy. Add hot milk, a little at a time, and whip until smooth, fluffy and of desired consistency. Whip in butter, a little at a time, until melted. Season to taste with salt and pepper. Makes about 6 servings.

New on cookbook shelves were **Adventures in the Kitchen** *by Spago's chef/owner Wolfgang Puck,* **Meatloaf** *by Sharon Moore,* **The Mediterranean Kitchen** *by Joyce Goldstein and* **In the Kitchen With Rosie: Oprah's Favorite Recipes** *by Rosie Daley.*

• 1990·1999 • 1990·1999 • FACTS •

Aromatic Vegetables and Rice

This dish fit the lifestyle of the health-minded vegetarians of the '90s. Low in fat and full of nutrients, it is hearty enough for a main-dish and sports a wonderful flavor.

1 tablespoon olive oil
1 cup chopped onion
2 cloves garlic, minced
½ teaspoon ground cumin
½ teaspoon ground cinnamon
¼ teaspoon ground ginger
1 can (14½ ounces) diced tomatoes, undrained
2 carrots, sliced
2 ribs celery, sliced
1 can (16 ounces) cannellini beans, drained, liquid reserved
½ cup water
1 cup frozen peas
1 zucchini, coarsely chopped
1 yellow summer squash, coarsely chopped
½ teaspoon salt
¼ teaspoon pepper
⅛ teaspoon hot pepper sauce
Cooked brown rice
Chopped parsley

Heat oil in a large skillet. Add onion and cook until almost tender. Stir in garlic, cumin, cinnamon and ginger. Cook, stirring, until fragrant, about 30 seconds. Add undrained tomatoes, carrots, celery, reserved liquid from the beans and water. Cover and simmer until carrots are almost tender, 10 to 15 minutes.

Add peas, zucchini, summer squash, cannellini beans, salt, pepper and hot pepper sauce. Cover and cook 5 minutes.

Serve over cooked rice, sprinkled with parsley. Makes about 6 servings.

Roast Pork Tenderloin with Fruit Salsa

1 pork tenderloin (12 to 16 ounces)
½ teaspoon sugar
1 teaspoon vegetable oil
½ teaspoon salt
¼ teaspoon pepper
¼ teaspoon ground coriander
1 tablespoon lime juice

Meat-loving Americans often looked to pork tenderloin during the '90s for their red-meat fix. It is lean and cooks quickly, two prerequisites during the decade. Americans also were salsa-happy, and when they tired of the traditional tomato variety they turned to a trendy fruit salsa.

Trim fat from tenderloin. Combine remaining ingredients and brush over all sides of the tenderloin. Let stand 30 minutes. Heat oven to 375°. Tuck thin end of meat under to make a roast of even thickness. Place in a shallow roasting pan and roast 35 to 45 minutes or until a meat thermometer registers 155°. Let rest 5 minutes, then slice crosswise. Serve with Fruit Salsa. Makes about 3 servings.

Fruit Salsa

1 medium papaya, peeled and chopped
1 mango, peeled and chopped
½ small green pepper, finely chopped
3 green onions, chopped
½ jalapeno pepper, seeded and minced
1 tablespoon lime juice
1 teaspoon honey
¼ teaspoon ground coriander
Salt to taste

Combine all ingredients and let stand at room temperature for 30 minutes or in the refrigerator for up to 4 hours. Serve at room temperature.

Sea bass was the haute fish of the '90s, and crusting it with nuts, potatoes or Japanese bread crumbs was de rigueur. Sea bass is not always readily available, but any other firm white fish can be substituted.

Pistachio-Crusted Sea Bass with Beurre Blanc Sauce

1 egg white
1 teaspoon cornstarch
½ cup ground pistachios
½ cup bread crumbs
Salt and pepper
4 sea bass steaks, 1-inch thick

Beurre Blanc Sauce
1 shallot, chopped
2 tablespoons white wine vinegar
½ cup dry white wine
½ cup whipping cream
1 cup (2 sticks) butter, cut into pieces
  and well chilled
2 tablespoons chopped chives

Beurre Blanc Sauce: Place shallot, vinegar and white wine in a medium saucepan and bring to a boil. Simmer until mixture has reduced to about 2 tablespoons. Add cream and continue to simmer until reduced again to about 2 tablespoons.

Easting Well, Cook's Illustrated *and* Saveur *magazines premiered;* Cook's *magazine folded.*

Reduce heat to low and add butter, one piece at a time, whisking just until it is incorporated before adding another. The sauce should be emulsified and creamy. Do not allow the sauce to get too hot or it will separate. Add chives and set over hot water to keep warm while preparing fish.

Beat egg white and cornstarch until cornstarch is dissolved and white is frothy. Combine pistachios, bread crumbs, salt and pepper.

Brush fish generously on both sides with egg white mixture. Coat with crumb mixture, pressing down so mixture adheres.

Place on a greased baking sheet and bake in a 400° oven for 8 to 10 minutes or until fish is cooked through. Spoon sauce on serving plates and top with fish. Makes 4 servings.

1990·1999 · FACTS · 1999·1990·1

McDonald's introduced the McLean Deluxe, a burger with a mere 10 grams of fat. Customers weren't impressed. Meanwhile, the Center for Science in the Public Interest analyzed the more popular Quarter Pounder and reported it contained 20 grams of fat.

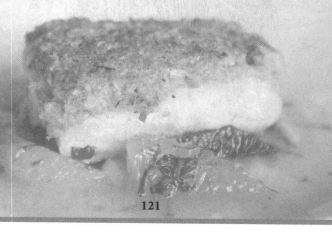

1990

Pillsbury awarded its first million-dollar prize at the Bake-Off in 1996. Kurt Walt of Redwood City, CA won the prize with this recipe. It was a recipe of the times, using two "light" ingredients and some timesaving convenience products.

Macadamia Fudge Torte

Filling
⅓ cup low-fat sweetened condensed milk (not evaporated)
½ cup semi-sweet chocolate chips

Cake
1 package (2-layer size) Pillsbury Moist Supreme Devil's Food Cake Mix
1½ teaspoons ground cinnamon
⅓ cup vegetable oil
1 can (15 ounces) sliced pears in light syrup, drained
3 eggs
⅓ cup chopped macadamia nuts or pecans
2 teaspoons water

Sauce
1 jar (17 ounces) butterscotch caramel ice cream topping
⅓ cup milk

Heat oven to 350°. Spray a 9- or 10-inch springform pan with nonstick cooking spray. In small saucepan, combine Filling ingredients; cook over medium-low heat until chocolate is melted, stirring occasionally.

In a large bowl, combine cake mix, cinnamon and oil. Blend at low speed for 20 to 30 seconds or until crumbly. (Mixture will be dry.)

Place pears in blender container or food processor bowl with metal blade; cover and blend until smooth.

In another large bowl, combine 2½ cups of the cake mix mixture, pureed pears and eggs. Beat at low speed until moistened. Beat 2 minutes at medium speed. Spread batter evenly in sprayed pan. Drop filling by spoonfuls over batter. Stir nuts and water into remaining cake mix mixture. Sprinkle over filling.

Bake for 45 to 50 minutes or until top springs back when touched lightly in center. Cool 10 minutes. Remove sides of pan. Cool 1½ hours or until completely cooled.

In a small saucepan, combine Sauce ingredients. Cook over medium-low heat for 3 to 4 minutes or until well blended, stirring occasionally. Just before serving, spoon 2 tablespoons warm sauce onto each individual dessert plate. Top each with a wedge of torte. If desired, serve with ice cream and garnish with chocolate curls. Makes 12 servings.

Molten Chocolate Cakes

½ cup (1 stick) butter
6 ounces good-quality bittersweet chocolate
1 tablespoon brandy
2 pasteurized eggs
2 pasteurized egg yolks
5 tablespoons sugar
1 teaspoon vanilla
Pinch of salt
2 tablespoons flour
Whipped cream for topping

Butter four 6-ounce ramekins. Place on a baking sheet.

Melt butter and chocolate together in the microwave or over very low heat, stirring constantly. Remove from heat and cool slightly. Stir in brandy.

Beat eggs, egg yolks, sugar, vanilla and salt until thickened and light, about 5 minutes. Fold in chocolate mixture and flour. Divide batter among prepared ramekins. (The cakes can be made a day ahead to this point, covered and refrigerated. Return to room temperature before baking.)

Heat oven to 400°. Bake cakes until tops are firm and puffed but centers are soft, about 15 minutes.

Cool cakes 2 minutes. Place an individual dessert dish over each ramekin and invert cakes. Let stand a few seconds, then remove ramekins. Serve warm with whipped cream. Makes 4 servings.

New York chef Jean-Georges Vongerichten gets credit for inventing these individual cakes with soft, rich centers. Some wonder if the cakes were an accident, unintentionally undercooked with still-runny centers. However they came to be, they caught on quickly late in the decade.

Because the cakes are only slightly baked, it is best to use pasteurized eggs in this recipe to ensure safety.

1990

It was the movie Sleepless in Seattle that brought this Italian dessert to Americans' attention. Few knew what it was or how to pronounce it, but recipes began appearing on the Web, and delis began offering it in their refrigerated cases. The name (pronounced TEE-ra-mee-SOO) means "lift me up." The dessert is rich and delightful – a sure mood lifter.

Tiramisu

6 egg yolks
1 cup sugar
⅔ cup milk
1 pound mascarpone cheese
1½ cups whipping cream
¼ cup strong brewed black coffee, cooled
¼ cup Kahlua or other coffee-flavored liqueur
2 packages (3 ounces each) ladyfingers, halved lengthwise
Cocoa for garnish

In a medium saucepan, beat egg yolks and sugar. Slowly beat in milk. Place over medium heat and bring to a boil, stirring constantly. Boil 1 minute or until thickened. Cool, then chill.

Add mascarpone cheese to the cooled egg mixture, whisking until smooth. Whip cream until stiff. Fold into cheese mixture.

Combine coffee and liqueur. Line bottom and sides of a 2½- to 3-quart bowl or springform pan with ladyfinger halves, split sides up. Drizzle generously with coffee mixture.

Spoon half of the cheese mixture over the ladyfingers. Repeat.

Cover and refrigerate at least 3 hours. Dust with cocoa to garnish. Makes 8 to 10 servings.

1990-1999 FACTS 1990-1999

The TV Food Network, a 24-hour food channel, made its debut in 1993.

The first fat-free "fat" hit the market with the introduction of Promise Ultra margarine.

124

Crème Brûlée

4 egg yolks
¼ cup granulated sugar
2 cups whipping cream
1 teaspoon vanilla
⅓ cup light brown sugar, sifted

As happens with many trends, this one started in restaurant kitchens. Although crème brûlée is an old classic, it resurfaced with gusto in the '90s. Rich and silky smooth, it is elegant in its simplicity.

Beat eggs yolk and sugar for 5 minutes, until light. Place cream in the top of a double boiler and place over direct heat until hot. Pour a little of the cream into the yolk mixture, beating constantly. Return all of the mixture to the double boiler and place over simmering water. Cook, stirring constantly, until hot and slightly thickened, but not boiling. Stir in vanilla.

Pour mixture into 6 to 8 ovenproof serving dishes. Refrigerate 6 hours or overnight.

Sprinkle sifted brown sugar evenly over the custards. Place about 4 inches from broiler heat source. Broil until sugar melts, 3 to 4 minutes. Watch carefully so sugar doesn't burn. Chill before serving. Makes 6 to 8 servings.

Nabisco took the world by storm when it introduced SnackWell's cookies and crackers in 1993. Fat-free or reduced in fat, the snacks were snatched off of supermarket shelves. Reports surfaced of consumers following delivery trucks to stores to ensure getting a supply. SnackWell's Creme Sandwich Cookie soon outsold Nabisco's Oreo cookie.

Index

Desserts	Era	Page